The 7 Deadly Sins of C

(Let's Get It Right Every Time)

Also by Elizabeth J Tucker:

Simply Stress (Stress Management Exercises, Strategies and Techniques)

The 5 P's For a Perfect Meeting (A Step-by-step Guide to Navigate Meetings Like a Pro)

Success Starts Here (Things Every Minute Taker Should Know)

Publisher: Shepherd Creative Learning

The 7 Deadly Sins of Chairing Meetings
(Let's Get It Right Every Time)
By: Elizabeth J Tucker

Copyright:

Publisher's Note:

The author has made every reasonable attempt to achieve complete accuracy of the content in this book prior to going to press. The publisher, the editor and the author cannot accept responsibility for any errors or omissions, however caused.

You should use this information as you see fit, and at your own risk. You should adjust your use of this information and recommendations accordingly.

Finally, use your own wisdom as guidance. Nothing in this Guide is intended to replace common sense, legal, or other professional advice. This book is meant to inform and entertain the reader.

No responsibility for loss or damage occasioned to any person acting, or refraining from action, as a result of the material in this publication can be accepted by the publisher, the author or the editor.

Dedication:

The book is dedicated to Dennis Shepherd (my lovely partner), and Rosemary Tucker and Geoffrey Tucker (my hugely supportive parents).

This book is also dedicated to all the people who have attended our Chairing Successful Meetings and Minute Taking Made Easy training workshops. It's also dedicated to all the chairmen and women that I've talked to in the course of my research. Thank you for sharing your views, experiences and questions to help make this book possible.

About the Author:

Elizabeth is based near the Cotswolds. She has several roles. Elizabeth is a successful author, business consultant, holistic life coach and stress management consultant.

Elizabeth is an innovative presenter with an engaging manner. She has spent many years helping individuals and organisations achieve their goals. Elizabeth writes her books based on her considerable business knowledge and experience.

She describes herself as an enthusiastic go-getter with a passion for helping others reach their full potential or achieve their goals. Elizabeth uses her own unique blend of insight, wisdom and humour in her work. Her catchphrase is "inspiration and support when you need it".

As well as a successful corporate career she has owned and managed several businesses. Since starting her own business in 2003 she has had the privilege of working with a diverse client base. Her clients have included The Chartered Institute of Housing, Blue Chip companies, the British Army, charities, social housing providers, SME and start-up businesses, and personal clients.

Elizabeth is currently working on a project to create a series of self-help business books. These will be available as paperbacks and Kindle books. You can find out when these are published by viewing her LinkedIn profile (liz-tucker/10/531/68/) or following her on Twitter (@liztucker03).

Table of Contents

PREFACE   10

1. INTRODUCTION   12
Exercise: The 7 Key Skills of a Good Chairperson   12
Exercise: The Worst Meeting Ever   15

2. FREQUENTLY ASKED QUESTIONS   18
3. TYPES OF MEETING   22
3.1 Formal Meetings   22
3.2 Business Meetings   23
3.3 Informal Meetings   24
Exercise: The Meetings I Chair   25

4. THE SKILLS AND BEHAVIOURS OF EFFECTIVE
CHAIRMEN/WOMEN   27
4.1 Skills of Effective Chairmen/Women   27
4.2 Behaviours of Effective Chairmen/women   28
Exercise: Evaluate Your Skills as a Chairperson   29
Exercise: Your Strengths and Weaknesses as a Chairperson   30

5. THE CHAIRPERSON'S ROLE   32
Exercise: Barriers to Good Meetings   32
5.1 Before the Meeting   33
5.2 During the Meeting   34
5.3 After the Meeting   36
Exercise: What Have I Learnt About the Chairperson's Role?   36

6. PLANNING THE MEETING   38
6.1 The Agenda   39
Exercise: My Criteria for Agenda Items   40
6.2 The Chairperson's Agenda   41
Exercise: My Chairperson's Agenda   42

7. GETTING PREPARED FOR THE MEETING   44
7.1 Chairperson and Minute Taker Briefing   44
7.2 Before the Meeting Starts   45
Exercise: Review of the Planning Stage   45

8. CHAIRING MEETINGS   47
8.1 Chairing Formal Meetings   47
8.2 Chairing Business Meetings   49
8.3 Chairing Informal Meetings   50

9. THE BUSINESS OF THE MEETING   51

Exercise: My Self Confidence 51
9.1 Opening the Meeting 52
9.2 Working Through the Agenda 53
Exercise: Any Other Business 56
9.3 Closing the Meeting 57
Exercise: Meeting Review 58

10. COMMUNICATION SKILLS 59
10.1 Verbal Communication 59
10.2 Questioning Skills 60
10.3 Active Listening Skills 61
10.4 Body Language 62
10.5 Dealing With Problem Attendees 62
Exercise: Assess Your Communication Skills 66
Exercise: Communication Skills Action Plan 67

11. NOTE TAKING AND RECORDING ACTIONS 69

12. APPROVING AND ISSUING THE MINUTES 70
12.1 Styles of Minutes 70
12.2 Approving the Minutes 71
12.3 Who Should Have a Copy of the Minutes? 72
Exercise: Review of the Meeting and Post-meeting Stage 72

13. FREEDOM OF INFORMATION ACT 74
13.1 The Public Sector 74
13.2 What is Covered by the Freedom of Information Act? 75
13.3 Exempt Information 75
13.4 Useful Websites 76

14. CONCLUSION 77
Exercise: Chairing Meetings Quiz 78
Exercise: Chairing Meetings Case Study 80

15. TERMS 85

16. APPENDICES 87
16.1 Exercise: The 7 Key Skills of a Good Chairperson - Answers 87
16.2 Exercise: Evaluate Your Skills as a Chairperson - Answers 87
16.3 Exercise: My Self Confidence - Analysis 88
16.4 Exercise: Assess Your Communication Skills - Answers 89
16.5 Exercise: Chairing Meetings Quiz - Answers 90

Preface

Are you brand new to chairing meetings, or are you an experienced chairman/woman? Have you attended a formal chairing meetings training event, or were you thrown in at the deep end?

In the course of my research, most of the chairmen/women I met had never received any formal training. Instead they developed their skills by watching and copying other chairmen/women. This is fine but it does mean you will pick up their bad habits as well as their good practices. This probably explains why 'Any other business' is often misused and abused by chairmen/women.

I've been involved with meetings for most of my adult life. My experience has included being an attendee, chairperson and minute taker. I've been involved in formal, business and informal meetings, so I know a thing or two about meetings.

Attending a formal chairing meetings training event is definitely beneficial to new chairmen/women. Not all organisations are willing to make this investment though. The good news is you can learn to be an expert chairperson without attending a formal training event. This is why I wrote The 7 Deadly Sins of Chairing Meetings (Let's Get it Right Every Time).

The topic of meetings is much broader than just chairing the actual meeting. This prompted me to collate my knowledge and expertise into a series of three books. The titles of the other two books in the series are:

1. The 5 P's For a Perfect Meeting (A Step-by-step Guide to Navigate Meetings Like a Pro). As the title suggests this book will guide you through the end-to-end meeting process.

2. Success Starts Here (Things Every Minute Taker Should Know). This practical guide deals with the role of the meeting secretary and the minute taker. It will help the reader to create clear, concise and accurate minutes time after time.

Each book is designed to be a practical guide. You will find handy hints and exercises throughout each book. The exercises will test your knowledge or provide you with an opportunity to think about how you and your organisation currently operate.

I wrote The 7 Deadly Sins of Chairing Meetings to address the common mistakes made by chairmen/women. With care and practice everyone can become an effective chairperson. The higher you climb up the career ladder the more important it is to demonstrate excellent chairing skills.

1. Introduction

We all have our own opinions about what makes someone a good chairman/woman. Interestingly, no two people will share exactly the same views. The one thing everyone agrees on is the chairperson is largely responsible for the success or not of the meeting. It really is a case of the buck stops here.

Of course there are many elements to successful meetings, but a key feature is effective communication. Professor Albert Mehrabian pioneered the Mehrabian Communication Model that is still used today.

Part of his research looked at the most effective means of communication (written, verbal and non-verbal). His research suggests the written word only carries 7% of the true meaning and feeling of the message. This immediately presents a case for face-to-face meetings or teleconferences.

His research then goes further to suggest that face-to-face meetings are more effective than teleconferences. According to his research only 38% of the meaning and feeling is carried verbally. He states that 55% of the meaning is carried by facial expressions and non-verbal communication.

Professor Mehrabian doesn't stop there. He goes on to suggest that typical video-conferencing is not as reliable as face-to-face communications. In fairness, technology has progressed in leaps and bounds since his original research.

The bottom line is meetings play an important role in modern businesses. Meetings are vital for effective leadership, business management, organisational productivity and good communication. However, when was the last time you heard someone say "that was a really good meeting"?

Whether your oganisation prefers face-to-face meetings video conferences or teleconferences someone has to chair the meeting. Being an efficient and effective chairperson is a skill. The good news is anyone can develop the skills needed.

Before we go any further you might like to consider the seven key skills of a good chairperson.

Exercise: The 7 Key Skills of a Good Chairperson

What do you think are the seven key skills all good chairmen/women share? Write your answers on a piece of paper.

You will find the answers to this exercise in the Appendices section at the end of the book. Compare your responses with the answers.

How did you fare? I hope you will find some useful nuggets of information in this book. My aim is to help you become an even more effective chairperson than you already are.

By the end of 'The 7 Deadly Sins of Chairing Meetings' you will:

1. Be able to chair formal, business and informal meetings

2. Recognise the skills and behaviours of successful chairmen/women. You will also be able to identify and plug your skills gaps

3. Develop strong time-management skills

4. Use assertiveness skills to navigate your way through meetings

Are you guilty of any or all of the seven deadly sins of chairing meetings? Here they are:

1. Time wasting:
Business time is expensive so use it wisely. Are all those meetings really necessary, or did they just seem like a good idea at the time?

2. Too many people or just the wrong people at the meeting:
It's tempting to invite people in case their input will be useful. However, this won't lead to a fruitful meeting. Make sure everyone has a useful contribution to make

3. Poor time management:
Do you start any of your meetings late? Do your meetings overrun and end late? Do you allow the discussion to continue until the topic has been exhausted?

4. An ineffective chairperson:
Do your meetings include the talkaholic, the non-contributors, more than one person talking at once, or heated disagreements? Need I say more?

5. No actions or not recording the actions properly:
Are your meetings just a talking shop? The aim is to achieve something, which means actions. Actions need to be properly recorded so they can be followed up

6. Late arrivals:
Aside from being disrespectful, late arrivals disrupt the flow of the meeting. Do you recap for late arrivals? In future adopt a zero tolerance attitude - don't arrive on time, don't attend

7. Electronic devices:

Electronic devices are a menace in meetings. Do attendees at your meetings check and/or answer emails and text messages? If so, they clearly aren't paying full attention to the meeting. Don't allow this bad practice to continue

On reflection, how productive are your meetings? How many of the deadly sins are you guilty of? It's worth addressing your bad habits as there are many advantages to properly run meetings.

First off, meetings save time, and increase staff motivation and productivity. Meetings are often used for problem solving, and are great for creating new ideas and initiatives. Most importantly, meetings prevent 'not invented here' syndrome and diffuse conflict in a way that emails cannot.

Of course if you are going to have a meeting it needs to serve a purpose. Most meetings should serve one of the following purposes:

1. Confirm what has already happened

2. Deal with current issues

3. Plan for the future

Each meeting has a beginning, middle and end. Good meetings constantly move forward towards the end. A bad meeting often arrives at the end more by accident than good leadership. Which camp do your meetings sit in?

It's been said many times before but, timing really is everything in a meeting. You may have meticulously planned your meeting but if you run out of time it will all have been for nothing. Whether you create the agenda or delegate the task do it with care.

When creating the agenda be totally realistic about what can be achieved in the meeting time available.

Do you know where to place contentious agenda items? People are at their most tense at the start of a meeting. Therefore, never start with a contentious topic. Instead sandwich it between bland or non-contentious matters.

Every meeting needs a chairperson, but not just anyone. It's important to choose someone who is going to be effective in this important role. Of course we all have to start somewhere. You may choose to allow your staff to start learning and practising their chairing skills at informal meetings. This is a good introduction into chairing meetings.

As the chairperson, your first task is to decide if a meeting really is necessary. It's too easy to opt for a meeting without thinking about whether it's the best option. Before deciding to have a meeting, ask yourself - "can the issues be resolved equally well without a meeting"?

Think about a meeting you attended recently. Did you come away feeling that was useful, or did you feel frustrated or even bored? Use your observations to reflect on the meetings you chair. Is there anything you can do to improve the quality of the meetings you chair? We can all learn from other people's mistakes if we feel inclined to do so.

Exercise: The Worst Meeting Ever

We've all sat through bad meetings; usually as an attendee. Perhaps the memory of it still sends shivers down your spine. Even a bad experience can be a blessing in disguise. You can use the experience as an opportunity to ensure you don't get the award for 'the worst meeting ever'

Instructions:

Think about the worst meeting you have ever attended as the chairperson or a contributor. Consider the following:

1. Write a list of all the things that made this meeting so bad and memorable

2. Was there anything that was good about this meeting? If so, make a note of what was good. Even bad meetings generally have some good points

3. When you chair meetings have you made any of the mistakes you identified in point 1? If so, what mistakes have you made?

4. What have you learnt from this exercise?

5. What are you going to do differently in future?

Let's be clear, not every meeting is bad and some are excellent. Most meetings fall into the category of OK but not something the attendees look forward to. There are some common reasons why meetings are not as effective as they could be:

Which of the following statements apply to you? Read each statement and select 'yes' or 'no':

1. I have no input into creating the agenda. I leave the meeting secretary to produce the agenda - Yes/No

2. My copy of the agenda is the same as everyone else's - Yes/No

3. I invite people to my meetings as they might be useful, or I feel I should invite them (office politics) - Yes/No

4. I don't brief the attendees on what is expected of them as I assume they already know - Yes/No

5. I only get the action updates when reach 'Matters Arising' in the meeting - Yes/No

6. I have a 'briefing' with the minute taker before my business meetings - Yes/No

7. I check what support the minute taker will need during the meeting - Yes/No

8. I start my meetings when everyone has arrived, rather than the published start time - Yes/No

9. I sometimes issue the agenda at the start of the meeting, or run business meetings without an agenda - Yes/No

10. I issue the minutes from the previous meeting at the start of the meeting - Yes/No

11. I recap for latecomers - Yes/No

12. I don't bother with introductions as this is a waste of meeting time - Yes/No

13. I lead every discussion in my meetings - Yes/No

14. I ignore private conversations or sub-meetings that take place during the meeting - Yes/No

15. I ignore multiple people speaking at once, and just try to talk over them - Yes/No

16. On occasions I have people present who don't contribute anything to the meeting - Yes/No

17. I occasionally have difficult people at my meetings. I ignore their poor behaviour as I don't want to give them special attention - Yes/No

18. I tell everyone that I value their contribution - Yes/No

19. I stop arguments as soon as they start - Yes/No

20. I allow each discussion to continue until we've exhausted the subject - Yes/No

21. Sometimes I forget to agree an action owner and/or completion date - Yes/No

22. Sometimes we give actions to people who aren't at the meeting - Yes/No

23. I expect the minute taker to know what needs to be minuted - Yes/No

24. I continue with the meeting until every agenda item has been discussed, even if this means the meeting finishes late - Yes/No

25. I use 'Any other business' to go around the table and get an update from everyone -Yes/No

26. I use 'Any other business' to discuss anything the attendees want to discuss -Yes/No

27. Sometimes I switch the order of the agenda during the meeting - Yes/No

28. Sometimes my meetings over-run, but this can't be helped - Yes/No

29. I sometimes make changes to the minutes before they're issued as I don't like the way they have been written - Yes/No

30. I don't always make reviewing the minutes a priority. Sometimes it takes a week or more before I review them - Yes/No

The majority of your answers should be 'No' to these questions. However, your answers to questions 6, 7, 18 and 19 should be 'Yes'.

How did you get on? This exercise is not a stick to beat yourself with. It's just an opportunity to identify some small changes you can make to improve your meetings.

2. Frequently Asked Questions

In the course of my research I talked to lots of people about their experiences of chairing meetings. Their feedback has been invaluable in creating this chapter. Here you will find the answers to the most frequently asked questions about chairing meetings.

Issue: Some people attend the meetings but don't say anything. What should I do about it?
Action: As the chairperson, it's your responsibility to deal with this. Make sure everyone makes a contribution to the meeting. Anyone who doesn't contribute should not be present at the meeting

Issue: I don't know who is responsible for creating the agenda for my meetings
Action: If you have a meeting secretary he/she will create the agenda on your behalf. As the chairperson, you may prefer to create the agenda yourself. Ask yourself 'is this a good use of my time'? You don't have to do everything yourself

Issue: I'm new to the organisation and have little knowledge of the meeting I will be chairing
Action: If possible attend your first meeting as an observer. Alternatively, ask the outgoing chairperson if you can work together for your first meeting

Issue: Should I introduce everyone at the start of the meeting?
Action: Ask the group if they all know each other. If they know each other there is no point in introductions. If they don't know each other make sure everyone introduces themselves. This is vital information for the minutes

Issue: Sometimes I find it difficult to know what has been agreed as there are lots of different ideas
Action: Stop the meeting and clarify. As the chairperson you need to be in control of your meeting. Your minute taker needs to understand what has been agreed, and may be relying on you to clarify this

Issue: Some people talk too fast and the minute taker struggles to keep up
Action: Ask everyone to slow down and only permit one person to speak at a time. Controlling the discussion is a key part of your role. Also, remember your role is to support your minute taker

Issue: I've noticed sometimes the discussion leaps from topic to topic. What should I do about this?
Action: This is your meeting. It's your job to make sure the discussion stays focused on the agenda item under discussion. You may need to be firm with some of the attendees. Trust me; the rest of the group will be grateful

Issue: Some of the discussions seem to be very lengthy. Should I just allow people to talk until we've covered everything?
Action: No. If the group is having a totally valid and useful discussion you may allow the matter to slightly overrun, but don't make a habit of this. It's important that you keep the discussion focused and relevant or you won't get through your agenda. Encourage people to summarise their input

Issue: Sometimes I have very disruptive people at meetings who ignore me when I try to bring the meeting to order
Action: As chairperson you can expel anyone who disrupts your meeting. Be firm about this. If you expel someone from the meeting don't back down as you will appear weak to the rest of the group. This could have a knock-on effect

Issue: I've noticed the same people seem to hog all the discussions. This is very irritating
Action: Aside from being irritating it means that you're probably missing a valuable contribution from other people. Your role is to encourage everyone to participate and manage those who hog the meeting. This role will develop your assertiveness skills

Issue: Sometimes the group returns to a matter already discussed
Action: As the chairperson, it's your job to keep the meeting moving forward. Don't allow the discussion to go backwards. The only exception is if something new and relevant has come to light

Issue: Sometimes we have too many agenda items. Do I finish the meeting on time and leave the outstanding items, or stay and finish the agenda?
Action: It's important not to overload the agenda in the first place. Calculate how long is needed for each agenda item, and how many items you can accommodate. Always finish the meeting on time. Any items not discussed should be given a priority listing at the next meeting

Issue: Do I need to approve the minutes?

Action: Yes. If you don't then the minute taker will have to issue them anyway, but they may contain factual errors. You can't amend the minutes after they have been issued so make this a priority task

Issue: I don't know when to approve the minutes. Does this form part of the next meeting?
Action: You should approve the minutes within five working days of the meeting (unless you meet weekly). By approving the minutes you are confirming they are an accurate record of your meeting. The rest of the group will have the opportunity to approve and adopt the minutes at the next meeting

Issue: Who is responsible for deciding who can have a copy of the minutes?
Action: You are. Everyone who was invited to the meeting is entitled to a copy of the minutes. Beyond that, it's a discretionary matter for you

Issue: Can I refuse to allow someone to attend my meeting?
Action: Yes. You are the chairperson and this is your meeting. It's part of your role to ensure you have the right people at your meeting, and everyone has a part to play. Never invite people 'just in case', or just because they want to be there

Issue: Do we need to follow the order of the agenda, or can I move things around during the meeting?
Action: It's important to follow the order of the agenda as this is all part of the audit trail. List the main agenda items in order of importance or the order you wish to discuss them

Issue: Sometimes people get nasty and make personal comments during meetings. Should I just ignore this and carry on, or say something?
Action: If you ignore it you just encourage this bad behaviour. Ideally you want to speak to the parties privately outside the meeting, but this isn't always possible. Everyone needs to understand that you won't tolerate bad behaviour in your meetings

Issue: The matters arising seem to take up most of our meeting. This leaves very little time for anything else
Action: You are allowing people too much time to deliver their updates. In most cases it should just be confirmation that the action has been completed. If the matter needs further discussion it should be listed as one of the main agenda items

Issue: I'm not sure whether I should include a comfort break in my meetings

Action: Where possible keep your meetings to less than two hours. Generally meetings of less than two hours don't include a comfort break. If your meeting is longer than this schedule a short comfort break. If you're going to include a comfort break be clear about how long you are allowing and restart the meeting at the appointed time (with or without all the attendees)

Issue: What should I do if have strong opinions about one of the agenda items?

Action: As the chairperson you should be impartial and objective at all times. If you wish to participate in one of the agenda items ask someone else to take the chair for that particular agenda item. Then you can be as partial as any other attendee as you're not acting as the chairperson

3. Types of Meeting

Meetings fall into three categories. These are formal meetings, business meetings and informal meetings. In your role as chairperson it's important to understand the type of meeting you are chairing. This will affect the way you conduct proceedings during your meeting.

3.1 Formal Meetings

There are lots of different types of formal meeting. I have provided a summary of the most common formal meetings for your information.

Annual General Meeting (AGM)
As the name suggests, this is an annual meeting. It's often a mandatory meeting, comprising the company's directors and shareholders. The chairperson will have been elected according to company rules. This is a very senior and responsible role.

Extraordinary General Meeting (EGM)
An EGM can be called at any time between AGMs if shareholder approval is required. The same rules apply to the meeting as apply to AGMs.

Board Meetings
A board meeting is attended by the board of a company or charity. The attendees are usually directors or trustees. These are often regular meetings, and the purpose is to discuss company business. If you are the chairperson for board meetings you will have been elected according to company rules.

A Standing Committee
A standing committee is a sub-committee of the company's board. This committee has delegated tasks, and meets regularly to discuss these. The committee can use its discretion to choose the chairperson.

One-off Committee
This committee is set up by the board to look at a single issue. The committee can meet as frequently or infrequently as they choose. The committee can use its discretion to choose the chairperson.

Public Meetings
As the name suggests, public meetings are open to anyone. Local government and private action groups often use this type of meeting. The committee leading the public meeting will select the chairperson.

Nominate a strong chairperson for this type of meeting as the public don't always know the rules of engagement in meetings.

Generally you won't know in advance how many people will be present at the meeting. This can be a little daunting for inexperienced chairmen/women.

Conference

Most conferences are private affairs but some are open to the public. The chairperson's primary role is often to act as a facilitator for the meeting.

Conferences generally involve several presentations, which are introduced by the chairperson. Although this style of meeting allows little room for discussion the chairperson may hold a question and answer session. He/she will invite questions from the audience and select one of the presenters to answer.

External Meetings

External meetings involve people from your own organisation along with representatives from outside the organisation. Due to the dynamics of the group you need to elect a strong and capable chairperson to run the meeting. Meetings that involve internal and external parties often involve hidden agendas.

3.2 Business Meetings

Business or workplace meetings are the most common form of meetings that most people chair. Business meetings are vital for effective leadership, business management and good communication throughout the organisation.

Not all business meetings are internal only. You may have business meetings with clients and/or suppliers. Treat these like any other business meeting.

Every business meeting you chair should serve a purpose. The first task is to identify why you need a meeting. Most organisations waste money on unnecessary business meetings each year.

Having decided a meeting is necessary your next task is to identify the aim and objectives of the meeting. Do this before considering who the attendees should be.

The more carefully you plan your meeting the more efficient and effective it will be. Always keep your meetings as small as possible but don't exclude people who can make a useful contribution.

Although business meetings generally involve a group of people you could have a one-to-one business meeting. Due to the nature of performance appraisals, a business meeting is ideal. It will provide the structure needed for this type of meeting.

You will find more information about the chairperson's role before, during and after the meeting in the chapter 5.

3.3 Informal Meetings

Just like formal meetings, informal meetings come in many guises. Whatever form your informal meeting takes make sure you do it away from your desk. Psychologically this makes it easier to end the meeting and walk away. Research shows that meetings around someone's desk tend to go on longer than necessary.

Even though you are having an informal meeting, think about location. A useful discussion is less likely if the attendees feel uncomfortable. Therefore, always opt for as much privacy as possible. This will encourage attendees to participate freely.

Whether your meeting is formal or informal, you still need a chairperson and, ideally, an agenda. A meeting without a chairperson becomes a free-for-all and generally lacks structure or direction. If you are chairing an informal meeting without an agenda use lots of eye contact. This will help you retain control of the meeting.

Here is a summary of the most common informal meetings.

Impromptu Meetings
This style of meeting can be very helpful for reaching decisions quickly. This is an ideal meeting for small groups that have an issue that needs a speedy resolution. Ideally you don't want a group size of more than four people for impromptu meetings.

Ideas Sharing Meetings
Some like to call these 'ideas sharing' meetings. Others prefer to refer to them as 'brainstorming' or 'thought showers'. Whatever you call it, they all amount to the same thing - a very short meeting for generating ideas.

For maximum impact these meetings should be no longer than 30-40 minutes and high energy. Throw an initial idea into the melting pot and then encourage a speedy flow of suggestions.

Ideas sharing meetings are good for creating new ideas or generating quick ideas for solutions to existing problems. Even though this is an informal meeting, still ask someone to make some notes. Otherwise the output is likely to be forgotten.

In order to make this type of meeting successful ensure the group consists of people with different expertise. Try to keep the group size small for the best results.

If you are chairing this style of meeting it's important not to criticise or judge the ideas presented. This would put people off contributing. The time for judging and feasibility is after the meeting. For now, just capture every suggestion with an open mind.

Informal meetings are often used for daily or weekly project planning, or progress updates. This style of meeting is excellent for keeping all team members informed.

If your informal meeting is likely to take more than 60 minutes consider scheduling a business meeting.

Exercise: The Meetings I Chair

As we've already discussed, meetings are expensive. Therefore, it's vital to ensure the right people attend your meetings. You will need a blank sheet of paper for this exercise.

Instructions:

1. Create two columns on your sheet of paper. In column 1 write the heading - 'Name of the Group or Meeting'. In column 2 write the heading - 'Attendees'

2. Identify all the groups or meetings you chair. Write this information in column 1

3. In column 2 write the names of all the attendees beside each meeting. Also write what each attendees brings to the meeting

4. Ensure there is a reason for people attending each meeting. If there's no reason or you discover they aren't really needed stop inviting them to future meetings

5. Finally, identify anyone who should attend your meetings but doesn't currently, for whatever reason

6. Create an action plan for future meetings

If the same group meets regularly it's a good idea to repeat this exercise at least once a year. It's very easy to get into the habit of inviting the same people even if they are no longer needed.

Note: this exercise is not intended as a stick to beat you with. Most people get into the habit of attending or chairing meetings but never question 'why'

.

4. The Skills and Behaviours of Effective Chairmen/women

Research suggests that meetings do a great deal to shape employees' attitudes towards the organisation. The success, or not, of a meeting is largely down to the skills and behaviour of the person chairing it. In short, the buck stops with you.

Most chairmen/women give presentations in the course of their work. No-one would ever expect to give a presentation without planning it. So, why do we think it's perfectly acceptable to chair a meeting without the same careful planning?

Chairing meetings requires a specific set of skills that need to be learnt and developed over time. Many organisations provide managers and staff with presentation skills training, but don't take the same approach to meetings. It's far too common to expect people to chair meetings with little or no training and support. These same organisations then complain when meetings are ineffective.

It's widely accepted that what sets effective chairmen/women apart from the others is a common set of skills and behaviours. Everyone can learn to be an expert chairperson if they put in the time and effort.

4.1 Skills of Effective Chairmen/Women

1. Good time management skills are one of the most important skills of an effective chairperson. This includes not overloading the agenda and managing the meeting time

2. Excellent communication skills. First, make sure you are clearly understood. Then deal with the attendees. Most people want to provide much more detail than time permits. Be assertive, not aggressive, in stemming their flow while ensuring they feel valued

3. Focused. Effective chairmen/women don't allow the meeting to drift away from the agenda or topic under discussion. Effective chairmen/women keep the meeting moving forward

4. The most effective chairmen/women are articulate. You need to be able to summarise the aim, objectives and outcomes of the meeting in terms everyone understands. Don't talk over people's heads. Clearly state your expectations at the start of the meeting

5. Presentation is important. The agenda needs to look neat, tidy and easy to understand. In short, it needs to look professional. White spaces are important in the agenda document

6. Assertiveness is a skill that is repeatedly used in effective meetings. You need to have the ability to challenge attendees in a non-threatening and non-aggressive way. You also need to be able to stop the meeting hog

7. Good leadership skills. If you have people at your meeting who aren't participating draw them into the discussion. This will demonstrate your leadership skills

8. Active listening skills are a must. See chapter 10 for more information on active listening

9. Assess the group dynamics. Understand the strengths and weaknesses of the group. Try to ensure the group comprises a mix of skills and knowledge

10. Timing your input is an acquired skill. It may influence the outcome of the discussion. Don't be tempted to put your opinion forward too early in the discussion. This may damage your credibility with senior personnel present

11. Keep the energy levels up. If all discussions become a series of negative comments the energy level will drop. Effective chairmen/women have the skills to keep the energy level up

12. Strong chairmen/women have the skills to deal with inappropriate behaviour

13. Ensure everyone feels valued for the contribution they have made

4.2 Behaviours of Effective Chairmen/women

1. Confidence (or giving the impressions of confidence) is essential in this role. The minute your colleagues sense doubt they will lose faith in everything you say; whether justified or not

2. If a question is asked, which you can't answer, throw it back to the group. This is known as deflecting or redirecting questions

3. Don't enter into an unofficial competition with other attendees. You need to remain impartial and objective, not try to outsmart other contributors

4. Effective chairmen/women genuinely welcome the diversity of views and contributions

5. Stimulate thoughts and relevant discussions during the meeting. This is partly down to assertiveness skills, but it's also an ability to think outside the box. If a discussion is slow to start or gets stuck, you may need to kick-start things

6. Effective chairmen/women don't allow the meeting to move forward until the action, action owner and completion date are captured

7. Good chairmen/women are able to manage their personal feelings. There will be people at your meetings that you don't like or rate professionally. Being able to manage your personal feelings is essential. Focus on the content, not the speaker or his/her behaviour

8. Learn from your mistakes. It takes a big person to admit they 'got it wrong' and learn from their mistakes

Exercise: Evaluate Your Skills as a Chairperson

Even the most effective chairmen/women have room for a little improvement. You might like to do this short exercise to evaluate your current skills as a chairperson.

Read each statement in turn and select the response that most closely relates to you. For example - "I invite everyone who may wish to contribute to my meetings to attend". Your answer may be 3. Be honest with yourself when evaluating your skills, but don't be overly critical.

1 = Never

2 = Occasionally

3 = Frequently

4 = Always

1. I only invite the people who need to attend my meetings

2. I appoint the minute taker before the meeting date so he/she can prepare for the meeting

3. I start every meeting on time, regardless of whether everyone has arrived or not

4. I explain the aim and objective of the meeting as part of my welcome (opening statement)

5. I approve or amend the minutes of the previous meeting before moving to the main part of the agenda

6. I stick to the order of the agenda

7. I give everyone a chance to contribute to the discussions, and actively encourage quieter members to speak

8. I know who the difficult attendees are (if any) and their hidden agenda

9. I ensure minutes or meeting notes are taken at every meeting

10. I agree the details of every action, action owner and completion date before the meeting moves on

11. I manage the timings to ensure all meetings finish on time

12. I ensure we agree the date, time and place of the next meeting before closing the current meeting

Now you have completed this self-assessment add up your score. Your score will be somewhere between 12 and 48. You will find the analysis for your score in the appendices section at the back of the book.

Exercise: Your Strengths and Weaknesses as a Chairperson

Now you have evaluated your skills as a chairperson and read the analysis, it's time to work on your strengths and weaknesses. Use the conclusions you draw from this exercise to create an action plan. You will need a blank sheet of paper for this exercise.

Instructions:

1. Get a sheet of paper and create two columns. In column 1 write the heading - 'My Strengths as a Chairperson'. In column 2 write the heading - 'My Weaknesses as a Chairperson'.

2. Start with your strengths; identify all the things you do well as a chairperson. For example, always start every meeting on time. Don't be too modest; it's important to recognise your skills

3. Now identify your weaknesses as a chairperson. Don't be judgemental; just write your observations down. If you are overly critical you will simply make yourself feel despondent, which is counter productive

4. Create an action plan for improving your chairing skills. This might include finding someone to mentor you, attending an assertiveness

training course, developing better organisation skills etc. The possibilities are endless

5. Set yourself a timescale for improving your skills. On the appointed date re-evaluate your chairing skills and reassess your strengths and weaknesses. Of course there is always room for improvement, but every chairmen/women is expected to demonstrate a basic level of competence

Handy hint: Every new chairperson needs help and support to become truly effective in this role. When you become an accomplished and respected chairperson consider mentoring new chairmen/women. You will both develop new skills - a win/win outcome.

5. The Chairperson's Role

Everyone realises that meetings require a chairperson. However, it's common for people to fail to recognise the other roles involved in meetings. There are potentially four roles involved in meetings. These roles are Chairperson, Minute Taker, Contributors and Observers.

Not every meeting will, or should, have observers. As the chairperson it's your responsibility to decide whether to allow observers at your meeting or not. To help you decide, observers are usually present for one of the following reasons:

1. He/she is a future minute taker for this meeting. It's good practice for the minute taker to observe one meeting before they take on the role of minute taker

2. He/she is a graduate, and attending this meeting as part of their professional development

3. The observer is your mentor, and is there to appraise your performance as a chairperson

Everyone else who attends your meeting should make a valuable contribution or not be there. As the chairperson, it's important that you ensure everyone understands what is expected of them.

As I've said before, the success, or not, of the meeting will be largely be due to you. We have all attended poor meetings and, hopefully, some good meetings. With some careful planning, proper preparation and good execution all meetings can be effective. Successful meetings are good for business.

Exercise: Barriers to Good Meetings

We all have our own ideas about what is a barrier to successful meetings. There are no right or wrong answers to this exercise. This is about your perception of good meetings.

Instructions:

1. Write down everything that you personally feel is a barrier to a successful meeting

2. Is there anything you can do about this (whether you're the chairperson or an attendee)?

3. Create an action plan for anything you can change or influence in future

You may like to revisit this exercise periodically. This will help ensure continuous improvement.

5.1 Before the Meeting

As the chairperson you will have already decided that a meeting is necessary. Hopefully you will have arrived at this decision objectively and not simply decided 'a meeting seems like a good idea'. Having decided that a meeting is the right option you now have several responsibilities before the event. These are:

1. Define the purpose and objectives of your meeting. If you can't do this you don't need a meeting

2. Decide what needs to be achieved at the meeting. For example, are there any decisions that must be taken? Meeting should never be just a talking shop

3. Decide how long is required for the meeting. This is essential to an effective meeting. This decision can be the typical 'chicken and egg' scenario. Do you decide how long to allow and then create the agenda according to the time available? Or, do you obtain the agenda items and then decide how long is needed?

This is your decision to make. Personally, I decide how long the meeting should be and then assess the value of the proposed agenda items. Some things just don't get included in the meeting as they aren't important enough

4. Identify who needs to attend the meeting. It's often tempting to invite people 'just in case' they are needed. Meetings are expensive so only invite those people who really are needed

5. Ask yourself "does everyone need to attend the entire meeting?" If someone has been invited to deliver a presentation they probably don't need to attend the entire meeting

6. Invite the attendees and explain what you expect them to contribute to the meeting. You can delegate this task to someone else, but it's important that attendees understand exactly what is expected of them

7. Identify if you need any visual aids, or other equipment, for your meeting

8. Appoint a minute taker. Don't make this decision at the start of the meeting as it's grossly unfair to the minute taker. It doesn't give him/her time to adequately prepare

9. Identify which style of agenda you want to use for this meeting. Note: the basic agenda is suitable for most business meetings

10. Make time to approve the agenda before it's issued

11. Arrange a Chairperson/Minute Taker briefing. This is an opportunity for both of you to confirm any help either of you requires during the meeting. For example, what to minute, managing the time etc

12. Identify which style of minutes you want the minute taker to create. It's essential the minute taker knows this in advance as this will dictate how detailed his/her notes need to be

13. Familiarise yourself with all the agenda items. You don't want to appear clueless during the meeting

14. Arrive in plenty of time to meet and greet all attendees and advise the minute taker of any last minute changes

Handy hint: When considering who to invite to the meeting think about the group dynamics. Small meetings make it easier to include everyone in the discussions. On the other hand, sometimes more views/input can be useful for complex problem solving. Just remember the more people who attend the more expensive the meeting gets and the less input everyone can have.

5.2 During the Meeting

Obviously your role during the meeting is essential. Without a chairperson the meeting will lack direction and may not cover all the topics listed on the agenda.

If the meeting is structured and well managed, expect no comments at all. If the meeting is anything less than orderly and focused you can be assured there will be plenty of criticism. Everyone has the skills to chair successful meetings, but it does take time, effort and practice. Knowing your responsibilities during the meeting is essential to success.

To clarify, your responsibilities during the meeting are:

1. Introduce everyone who has not attended previously, including visitors. This stops attention being diverted to trying to identify who everyone is

2. Explain the purpose of the meeting and any expected outcomes. Everyone should already know this. However, this is a useful way of getting attendees focused on the matters to be discussed

3. Ensure the agenda, and timings, are adhered to. This is important if you want a meeting that is a good use of company time and money

4. Don't allow any discussions that aren't on the agenda unless they are pre-agreed matters for Any other business

5. Good time management is absolutely essential to successful meetings. It's far too easy to allow discussions to drift on, but this impacts the rest of the meeting

6. Ensure only one person speaks at a time. It's very difficult for the minute taker to follow the discussion if multiple people are speaking at once

7. Ensure all attendees have the opportunity to make a useful contribution to the meeting

8. Manage difficult attendees and don't allow anyone to hijack the meeting

9. Be aware of anyone who isn't contributing to the meeting. Draw him/her into the discussions

10. Value everyone's contribution. This will help draw shy attendees out of their shell

11. Encourage a free exchange of views but in a non-critical way. The best ideas and solutions arise when everyone feels comfortable contributing

12. If anyone is rambling on, politely stop them. You don't have time for rambling in a meeting

13. Resolve arguments quickly. Failure to do so is likely to result in people making personal and offensive remarks. Find some merit in each side of the argument

14. Be aware of any help the minute taker needs. You may need to confirm what should be minuted, or slow the discussion down so he/she can keep up

15. Keep everyone focused on the purpose of the meeting and the item under discussion

16. If any of the discussions have been lengthy, summarise the discussion before moving on

17. At the end of the meeting, remember to thank everyone. This small gesture makes people feel valued, which is important for the success of future meetings

Handy hint: Attendees who don't contribute to the meeting should either start participating or leave. If they have nothing to contribute they don't need to be wasting company time and money attending the meeting. The only exception is observers.

5.3 After the Meeting

Although the minute taker has the largest workload following the meeting, you have a role to play too. Your responsibilities are:

1. Provide any support the minute taker needs to create a clear, concise and accurate set of minutes

2. Approve the minutes as soon as possible. It's good practice to approve the minutes within two working days of receiving them. The minute take should issue the minutes within five working days of the meeting

3. Do not feel tempted to amend the minutes unless the content is factually incorrect. It's very tempting to apply your personal writing style to the document, but don't. Minutes are a factual record of the meeting, not an opportunity for personal writing styles

4. If you work in the public sector consider the Freedom of Information Act when reviewing the minutes

5. Be prepared to support the attendees in completing their actions, if necessary

6. Confirm who is entitled to a copy of the minutes. Anyone who was invited to the meeting is entitled to a copy of the minutes. Anyone else must obtain your permission as this was your meeting

Exercise: What Have I Learnt About the Chairperson's Role?

Before moving on you might like to evaluate what you've learnt about the chairperson's role.

Instructions:

Consider the following questions.

1. Is there anything you didn't already know about the chairperson's role? Think about the tasks before, during and after the meeting

2. Create a list of what you've learnt

3. Is there anything you will do differently in future? If so, what?

Recognising what you've learnt from something can be a great motivator to encourage further learning. Hopefully this exercise will inspire you to read the rest of the book.

6. Planning the Meeting

Good meetings don't just happen by accident. They are the result of careful planning and good organisational skills.

Before rushing off to plan the agenda for your meeting stop and ask yourself if a meeting is necessary. During the planning stage of a meeting you need to consider each of the following:

1. A meeting is necessary (not, 'it just seems like a good idea')

2. The person calling the meeting has a clear aim and objectives in mind

3. The right people are invited to the meeting, and everyone has a part to play. The chairperson is clear about what is expected of everyone

4. An appropriate venue has been selected. Meetings around someone's desk are rarely satisfactory

5. Enough, but not too much, time has been set aside for the meeting. You need to decide how long is enough meeting time

6. Having decided to go ahead with a meeting you have a well thought out agenda. This is essential if you want to get the maximum benefit from the meeting

7. The chairperson and minute taker have been selected. Doing this at the start of the meeting will not give them time to prepare properly

Having identified that a meeting is necessary decide whether this is to be a formal, business or informal meeting. This will dictate how you plan it. There is no substitute for good planning.

Before you set to work on the agenda consider the aim and objectives of your meeting. You need to be very clear about the purpose of the meeting and what you need to achieve. If you can't articulate this clearly and easily you don't need a meeting. This simple step could save you a lot of time and money.

Next, think about who to invite. Everyone who comes to the meeting should have a useful contribution to make. Never invite people just in case they might be needed, or because you feel obliged to.

Decide how many people should be invited. Small meetings allow everyone to contribute, whereas large meetings limit input. Sometimes a larger group is required because of the diversity of agenda topics. Decisions, decisions...

Now consider, does the meeting need to be face-to-face? Would videoconferencing work for your meeting? Do you want a combination of people present and some joining remotely? Do you have the facilities and equipment to accommodate this? These things need to be considered before you move forward with planning your meeting.

If everyone works in the same office then it's logical to have a face-to-face meeting. If some invitees work in different parts of the country, or even overseas, it may not be cost-effective for them to attend.

Only when all of these issues have been resolved are you ready to start planning the agenda.

6.1 The Agenda

An agenda is a plan of the topics to be discussed at your meeting. However it looks the agenda is an essential part of every successful meeting. A meeting without a well-planned agenda will lack structure and direction. It may even waste company time and money.

Creating an agenda forces you, the chairperson, to consider why you are having a meeting. It also makes you think about what you want the meeting to achieve, who should attend and how long is needed.

You may choose to create the agenda yourself, although most people delegate this task to a meeting secretary. You need to decide whether you want a basic agenda, full agenda or objectives agenda. If it's any help, a basic agenda is suitable for most business meetings.

Regardless of which style of agenda you opt for, the order of agenda items remains the same. The order for agenda items is always the same (see example below).

Name of the group that is meeting

Date and start time of the meeting

Full meeting address (this is to provide an accurate record for future audit purposes)

Apologies

Welcome (this includes housekeeping and introductions)

Minutes of the previous meeting

Matters arising (these are the actions from the previous meeting)

Reports (these are reports that don't form part of the main agenda items)

Main agenda items (listed in the order you wish to discuss them)

Any other business

Date of the next meeting

Handy hint: Although apologies appear on the agenda they are not given an agenda item number. 'Apologies' is only listed to act as a reminder for people to send their apologies if they won't be attending.

Exercise: My Criteria for Agenda Items

You may choose to delegate the task of creating the agenda to the meeting secretary. This is absolutely fine, but he/she needs some guidance on what should be included on the agenda. This decision is yours.

Instructions:

Before you go any further, consider the following:

1. Do you always accept every agenda item that is submitted?

2. What is your criterion for including an item on the agenda? If you don't set criteria then you could potentially end up with a mishmash and some irrelevant agenda items

3. How do you let people know if their agenda item isn't going to be discussed at the meeting?

4. When you accept agenda items do you tell the attendee how long they have to discuss their matter? Do you ask attendees how long they need to discuss the matter?

5. If you do neither of these how do you decide how long is required to cover the topic?

6. How do you communicate all of this to the meeting secretary?

7. What are you going to do differently in future?

By considering these questions and addressing any issues you automatically improve the quality of the meetings you chair.

6.2 The Chairperson's Agenda

This is sometimes referred to as the chairperson's brief. The chairperson's copy of the agenda is more detailed than the one issued to other attendees.

The chairperson's agenda includes details of the desired outcome for each agenda item. It also contains any background information that might be helpful to you during the meeting.

Below I have listed some typical outcomes that often appear the on the chairperson's copy of the agenda. You may or may not choose to use these for your meetings; it's a matter of personal choice:

1. Decision required

2. Discussion only

3. Share information with the group

4. Planning. This may involve a workshop session or agreeing plans for a project

5. An ideas generating discussion only

6. Obtain feedback regarding an action, event or outcome

7. Find solution to a problem

8. Agree targets, budgets, aims etc

9. A policy statement to be shared with the group

10. Team building or motivation

11. Guest speaker. Note: guest speakers are usually there to discuss something that doesn't normally feature as part of the meeting

Timings on the chairperson's copy of the agenda are useful. This will enable you to manage the discussion time more effectively. Most chairmen/women don't include timings on the agenda issued to attendees as it can be a distraction. Good timekeeping is essential if you want a successful meeting.

Add the timings when creating the agenda, not afterwards. This will enable you to see what can realistically be achieved in the time available to you. This is just another piece of the jigsaw puzzle that ensures you chair an effective meeting.

Here is an example of two items on the chairperson's agenda:

10.45 4. Staff for the new community office

Discuss the staffing level required for the new community office (All). Confirm the set up costs (FF)

Select a project owner to oversee the new office opening (All)

11.05 5. Maternity cover for Betty McBricker

Discuss plans for Betty McBricker's maternity cover. Are we going to recruit someone on a short-term contract or use agency staff to provide maternity cover? (BR)

We need to make a decision at this meeting as Betty McBricker will be leaving in 8 weeks' time

As you can see, this is much more detailed that the agenda you would issue to attendees. Having a detailed agenda like this means you don't have to try to remember everything.

Exercise: My Chairperson's Agenda

Do you currently use a chairperson's agenda for your meetings? Think about how useful this document is, or could be during your meetings.

Instructions:

Whether you currently use a chairperson's agenda or not, consider the following.

1. What information do you currently include on your chairperson's agenda?

2. Do you refer to this information during the meeting?

3. Will you change your chairperson's agenda for future meetings? If so, what will you change?

4. If you've never had a chairperson's agenda before, are you going to start creating one for your meetings? How do you think this will improve your chairing skills?

5. How does, or can, the chairperson's agenda make you a more effective chairperson?

Most chairmen/women delegate all the other planning tasks to a meeting secretary. This may include booking the meeting room, refreshments, parking spaces, inviting attendees etc.

Handy hint: You or the meeting secretary can invite people to your meeting. However, It's your responsibility to ensure everyone knows what is expected of them.

7. Getting Prepared for the Meeting

Meetings are deemed to be 'regular' or a 'one-off'. A regular meeting is any group that meets more than once. When deciding to schedule a meeting it's important for you, the chairperson, to decide which category the meeting falls into.

Everyone needs to know why he/she has been invited. As the chairperson it's your decision to invite the attendees, and your responsibility to explain your expectations of each attendee.

This simple act is often overlooked. By explaining why they have been invited and your expectations, everyone has an opportunity to prepare for the meeting. Doing this will improve the efficiency of your meetings.

To help the attendees prepare ensure everyone receives the agenda and other documents at least four working days before the meeting.

7.1 Chairperson and Minute Taker Briefing

It's good practice for the chairperson and minute taker to have a short briefing before the actual meeting. The day before is the ideal time for this briefing. Many chairmen/women don't make the time for this essential pre-meeting; believing that it's an unnecessary waste of time. Wrong!

This briefing can be completed in the time it takes to drink a cup of coffee. It can make the difference between an efficient or an average to poor meeting. The purpose of this short briefing is to ensure both parties are properly prepared. No chairperson likes nasty surprises during their meeting.

The purpose of this meeting is to discuss the following:

1. Any help or support either of you may need during the meeting

2. Decide who will be responsible for time-keeping

3. Discuss the agenda items. Does the chairperson wish to be prompted regarding any of the agenda items?

4. Are there any contentious or sensitive items on the agenda? If so, decide how these will be minuted

5. Are there any difficult or challenging attendees coming to the meeting? Do you have a strategy for dealing with them?

6. Does the minute taker know what to minute? Is the minute taker new to the role? If so, he/she may need you to dictate what should be minuted

7. Are there any updates on the matters arising? Ideally you should already have the updated actions from the last meeting

8. If you haven't already done so, tell the minute taker the style of minutes you require from this meeting. Your choices are summary, verbatim or action point minutes. For most business meetings summary minutes are the preferred choice

9. Confirm if you want a register for signing at the meeting. Also confirm if you want a copy of the minutes to sign at the meeting

Handy hint: It's common for the chairman/woman to ask the minute taker to be responsible for timekeeping.

7.2 Before the Meeting Starts

It's good practice for the chairperson and minute taker to arrive approximately 15 minutes before the rest of the attendees. This gives you chance to ensure the room is set up correctly and discuss any last-minute changes.

If you have external people or new attendees coming to the meeting, it's courtesy to be there to meet and greet them. This is also an opportunity for the you and minute taker to ensure you know who everyone is. This will help the meeting run smoothly.

You and minute taker should either sit side-by-side or somewhere you can easily make eye contact with each other. The success of the meeting will be partly due to how well you and the minute taker work as a team.

By arriving early you have an opportunity to decide where you want to sit. Do you want to sit at the head of the table or somewhere in the middle? There are pros and cons to both options, so this is a matter of personal choice.

Exercise: Review of the Planning Stage

Having gone through the complete cycle of the planning stage now is a good time to take stock. Consider what you currently do or don't do, and what you will do differently in future.

Instructions:

Consider the following questions:

1. Thinking about the agenda, how much thought do you put into planning the agenda currently?

2. Can you see ways you can improve the process for creating the agenda? If so, what?

3. What have you learnt about creating the agenda or the chairperson's agenda?

4. Are you always as well prepared for your meetings as you could be? If not, what could you do to prepare better?

5. Other than informal meetings do you always make time for a chairperson/minute taker briefing? If not, why not?

6. Do you put as much effort into the planning stage of your meetings as you do chairing the meeting? If not, why not?

7. When planning future meetings is there anything you will do differently? If so, what?

Create an action plan for anything you plan to do differently in future. Pilot your new working practices and see what does/doesn't work.

You may need to review and tweak the planning phase until you arrive at something that works for you.

8. Chairing Meetings

The way you chair formal, business and informal meetings will vary. In order to be an effective chairperson it's important that you understand the difference between these types of meetings.

Although the way these meetings are chaired varies you should remain calm, objective and impartial at all times. This is one of the key skills of a good chairperson.

8.1 Chairing Formal Meetings

The chairperson's role is significant in formal meetings. This is a serious and important role. Everyone attending the meeting will have great expectations of the ability of the chairperson.

In public companies the chairperson will be selected and controlled by company rules. A government committee selects its chairperson in accordance with statutory regulations.

As chairperson, one of your main responsibilities is ensuring the meeting is properly convened. You will need to ensure the meeting is quorate. You will find an explanation in the terms below. If the group isn't quorate you won't be able to make binding decisions.

Due the formal nature of this type of meeting you will always have a minute taker. Furthermore, you will probably use terminology that isn't used at other types of meeting.

There are various common meeting terms that are used in formal meetings. These terms are not generally used in business meetings. As the chairperson you are expected to know, and correctly use, these terms.

Adjourn = A suggestion to postpone the meeting to a future date. It's a good idea to agree the new date before everyone leaves the meeting room

Ad-hoc = A committee or group that is brought together for a specific task. This group will not have a regular meeting pattern

Advisory = A committee formed to give advice and/or recommendations. This committee cannot make binding decisions

Amendment = A change made to the minutes after they have been issued. This decision will be made when discussing the minutes of the previous meeting

Executive = A sub-committee with the power to make binding decisions on behalf of the entire committee/group. The executive is generally made up of the chairperson and other key personnel from the group

Motion = A formal proposal or recommendation from a member of the group. This usually requires a proposer and seconder before it can be voted on. Typically this is used at AGMs to elect or re-elect members. The proposer starts by saying "I move that..."

Note: all motions should be minuted. If possible, get the motions in writing before the meeting. This will help you during the meeting and make the minute taker's role easier

Motion Defeated = The majority of members have voted against a motion. As chairperson, you will announce the motion is defeated

Order of Business = A set procedure for very formal meetings. This is a term sometimes used by local authorities and trade unions

Plenary = This is a power that has been granted to a group with no limitation upon their power. They are permitted to make binding decisions on behalf of the group or organisation they are acting for

Point of Order = A discussion point that is made but is not relevant to the discussions. This term is used when one of the group wishes to be pedantic on a particular point or choice of words

Postal Votes = As the name suggests these are votes received via the post. Postal votes are only permitted if the constitution allows for them

Proxy = This is a vote made on behalf of a member who is absent. The absent member gives someone permission to cast their vote in their absence. Proxy votes are only permitted if the constitution allows for them

Quorum = The minimum number of members required for decisions made by the group to be binding. As the chairperson, It's your responsibility to know how many members are required for the group to be quorate. This is usually, but not always, a third of the group

Resolution = This is a decision to accept or reject a motion or suggestion from a member of the group. If the motion is passed it becomes a resolution

Rider = This is an addition to be made to a resolution once it has been passed by the members

Standing = A gathering of members who meet regularly

Standing Orders = Rules regarding how the meeting should be run

Sub-committee = A small committee from members of the group. A sub-committee is usually formed with a specific remit

Tabling Papers = These are documents that weren't circulated to the members prior to the meeting. Try to discourage this as you probably haven't allowed extra time to read and deal with these documents

Voting Rights = This is how the voting is done at formal meetings. This can be 'voice vote, a show of hands or a ballot'. A ballot is often used for electing officers if there is more than one nomination

Note: in the event of a tied vote the chair has the casting vote. If there is a clear winner, without the need for a casting vote, the chairperson may decide not to vote

Waiver = A rule that can be invoked to allow a mistake (usually procedural) to be overlooked

If you chair formal meetings but can't remember all of these terms, write them down.

8.2 Chairing Business Meetings

A business meeting is a halfway house between a formal and informal meeting. Most internal meetings and supplier or customer meetings fall into this category.

A business meeting has a chairperson (usually the person who decided to call the meeting), a minute taker, and attendees. You may also occasionally have observers at business meetings.

Chairing business meetings is the most common form of chairmanship. Your role is to lead the meeting and ensure it achieves its objectives and reaches its conclusion on time.

As the chairperson you can exert your influence over the meeting, although you must appear impartial and objective at all times. As the chairperson you have the casting vote if it becomes necessary. Try not to make your comments/observations until everyone else has spoken. Otherwise you may appear to be trying to influence proceedings. Your role is to facilitate the discussions but not lead them to your chosen conclusion.

As your role is one of leadership your input into the discussions should be neutral. If you have strong views and wish to robustly present your views ask someone else to chair the relevant agenda item. For this agenda item you will then be treated like any other attendee.

8.3 Chairing Informal Meetings

Your informal meeting may not have an 'official' chairperson but someone needs to lead the meeting. Ideally the unofficial chairperson should be selected before the meeting starts.

Informal meetings provide the ideal opportunity for new chairmen/women to learn and practice chairing skills. It's unfair to throw people in at the deep end by expecting them to instantly be an effective chairperson for business meetings.

At informal meetings the chairperson's role is to ensure every point of view is heard. As chairperson you must appear unbiased. This often means you can't participate fully in the discussions.

You can still exert your influence over the meeting though. To do this, allow detailed discussion of some issues and limited consideration of others. This will demonstrate that you're leading this informal meeting.

As the chairperson it's important that you block any negative tactics employed by other attendees. If you fail to stop this behaviour you are likely to end up with a 'meeting bully'. This person often uses their bullying tactics to get the outcomes he/she wants.

Just because this is an informal meeting, don't view your role as less significant than at any other meeting. Treat the task of chairing just as seriously.

Even if you decide against having an agenda you should have list of matters to be discussed at the meeting. This will keep everyone focused and prevent the meeting becoming a talking shop only.

Consider asking someone to make notes of the discussion and actions.

9. The Business of the Meeting

How a meeting starts is a good indication of its likely success. This is one reason why starting on time is so important. Pacing the meeting correctly and adhering to the order of the agenda are also important elements of effective meetings.

Ending the meeting late is almost certain to antagonise attendees, which may then harm your personal brand. If you get labelled as an ineffective chair this is a hard perception to change.

Handy hint: Never issue the agenda at the start of the meeting, or worse still run the meeting without an agenda. Both will result in no-one being properly prepared.

How confident do you feel chairing meetings? Some people love it; they see themselves as an actor on the stage. Others feel uncomfortable as they see this as a task they just have to get through.

Do you arrive at the meeting hugging your papers to your chest, head down and muttering a greeting? Or, do you walk in head held high, looking confident and relaxed?

The more confident you appear the more assertiveness and leadership skills you will demonstrate. Walk into the meeting looking organised, making eye contact, a friendly smile and a greeting. Research shows you will get better results.

People attending your meeting will feel much more positive about it, even though the meeting hasn't started yet. Even at this stage attendees are judging whether this is likely to be a good or bad meeting.

Exercise: My Self Confidence

How confident are you? Which of these approaches best describes you? Perhaps you have never considered this before, but think about it now as it can help you in the future.

Instructions:

Consider the following questions. Answer - yes, no or sometimes.

1. Do you feel comfortable making eye contact with people when you greet them? This applies to any situation, not just meetings?

2. At the start of your meetings do you scan the entire group to establish your presence and acknowledge them? Note: you only need to spend a few seconds on each person to do this

3. In general, do you sit with your head up and shoulders relaxed?

4. Do you make people feel you are interested in them/what they have to say by smiling at them?

5. Do you respond to everyone who speaks in your meetings?

6. What have you learnt about yourself from this exercise?

You will find the analysis for this exercise in the Appendices at the end of the book.

Having identified how confident you appear to others it's time to move on to the actual meeting.

9.1 Opening the Meeting

This is your meeting, and it's important that you demonstrate that you are in control from the outset. Things to consider when opening your meeting:

1. Start the meeting on time. Don't be tempted to wait for late arrivals. Delaying the start of the meeting suggests the late arrivals are more important than those who arrived on time

2. Ask everyone to switch off their mobile phones and other electronic devices. Mobile devices can be a distraction during the meeting

3. Deal with any other housekeeping matters e.g. fire exits, toilets, coffee machine etc

4. Summarise the aims and objectives of your meeting. This will help to get everyone focused on the meeting. Note: your opening statement should be a maximum of two minutes

5. Make it clear what decisions must be reached during this meeting. It's important to manage expectations at the start of the meeting as this helps to get everyone focused

6. Identify any confidential matters on the agenda

7. State any ground rules e.g. everyone's opinion is equally important, everyone will be treated with courtesy and respect etc

8. Confirm the finish time of the meeting, unless everyone already knows this

9. Do not acknowledge late arrivals as this disrupts the flow of the meeting. Just carry on as if you were unaware of them arriving late. This is a subtle way of marking your displeasure at their poor time-keeping skills

10. Never recap for late arrivals. If attendees don't arrive on time it's their responsibility to try to catch up. If you keep recapping for each late arrival your meeting will seriously over-run

The procedure for formal meetings is slightly different to that of business and informal meetings. In formal meetings make the introductions and then state "I would like to call the meeting to order. The main purpose of today's meeting is...."

Regardless of the type of meeting, as the chairperson you will be involved in every stage of the meeting. It's your job to introduce each agenda item in turn. This helps assert your position as chair of the meeting. You should not try to influence the outcome for any of the agenda items though.

9.2 Working Through the Agenda

There is an accepted order for agenda items. This doesn't vary from organisation to organisation. The order of the agenda is listed below.

Introductions and Welcome
Use this agenda item to remind everyone of the purpose of the meeting and what you need to achieve. This will help to get everyone focused. Also deal with any housekeeping matters now.

Ask everyone to introduce themselves if you have new attendees present. This is helpful to everyone at the meeting, especially the minute taker as he/she needs to record who was present.

Ask for any apologies so these can be recorded in the minutes.

Declarations of Interest
A declaration of interest is a potential conflict of interest relating to one (or more) of the agenda items. Attendees are required to declare any potential conflicts of interest. As the chairperson, it's your job to make sure they don't participate in the relevant discussions.

It's good practice for the chairperson to canvass any declarations of interest as part of the welcome and introductions. Not all chairmen/women think to do this.

Internal meetings rarely involve declarations of interest. However, declarations of interest may be raised in meetings involving external parties, board meetings and commercial meetings.

If anyone declares a conflict of interest in your meeting ask the minute taker to capture this for the minutes.

Minutes of the Previous Meeting

Before getting into the business of this meeting, It's good practice to finish the housekeeping for the previous meeting. Ask everyone present to confirm the minutes are an accurate record of the previous meeting. If so, you can formally adopt the minutes. Some organisations like to sign the minutes, not just approve them. Know your organisation's policy regarding this.

If the minutes are inaccurate this is the time to amend them. Everyone present needs to be in agreement with the proposed changes. The minutes should not include action updates or anything that wasn't discussed at the last meeting. Note: the minutes should not be amended for grammar or spelling mistakes.

Matters Arising

This is an important part of the meeting, and should be given sufficient time. Some chairmen/women allow this part of the meeting to take too long however. Each update should take less than 2 minutes. Don't allow attendees to waffle.

As the chairperson you should already be aware of what everyone is going to say during this agenda item. This will help ensure an efficient meeting.

Work through each action from the previous meeting in order. The action owner should provide a 'brief' update and confirm whether the action is now complete or not. If not, confirm what is still outstanding and when the action will be completed.

Don't allow actions to keep being carried forward and never completed. If any outstanding actions will be discussed as part of the main agenda deal with them under the main agenda item.

Reports

The report(s) should have been issued with the agenda. Anything presented under this agenda item is not a matter for discussion. Your role is to enquire whether there are any queries relating to the report(s). Only issues or queries relating to the report should be discussed at this point.

Do not encourage attendees to introduce new reports to the meeting. You haven't scheduled the time for people to read and respond to reports.

This agenda item should be dealt with very quickly. If a report is going to be discussed it should appear under the 'Main agenda items' not 'Reports'.

Main Agenda Items

The main agenda items should already have been listed in order or importance or the order you wish to discuss them. If you run out of meeting time the important matters will have been discussed. Anything outstanding can be carried forward to the next meeting.

Where necessary, provide an opening statement and confirm what needs to be achieved. Deal with each item in the order they appear on the agenda. The main agenda items are the key part of your meeting. Your role is to:

1. Introduce each agenda item

2. Invite the person leading the discussion to put forward their comments first

3. Invite input from the rest of the group

4. Manage everyone's contribution. You want to ensure that everyone contributes but no-one hijacks the meeting

5. Manage the timing of the discussion (unless you have delegated the task to someone else)

6. Summarise what needs to be minuted (if the minute taker needs help)

7. Confirm the actions, action owner and timescale for completing the actions

Any Other Business

This is the most misunderstood and abused part of meetings. This is largely because the chairman/woman and attendees don't understand the purpose of 'Any other business'.

Any other business is:

1. Not an opportunity to go around the table getting a personal update from each attendee

2. Not an opportunity to discuss any topic the group wants to talk about

3. Not an opportunity to discuss any agenda items members forgot to submit on time

So, what is the purpose of 'Any other business'? It's an opportunity to discuss urgent items that came to light after the agenda was issued. For example, a health and safety issue, a board decision that must be discussed etc.

Under normal circumstances you should have nothing to discuss under this agenda item. It should be the exception rather than the norm to have matters to discuss under 'Any other business'. Remember you haven't scheduled time for a lengthy discussion under this agenda item.

As the chairperson you have the right to refuse any requests for matters to be discussed under 'Any other business'. If you accept a matter under this agenda item, you and the minute taker should already know what it is. It's not acceptable for people to raise anything when the meeting reaches this point.

If you allow the group to randomly add 'Any other business' agenda items your meetings will not finish on time. This is one of the primary reasons for inefficient business meetings.

If you don't allow an item under 'Any other business' suggest it's added to the agenda for the next meeting.

Before closing a formal meeting, ask "are there any other matters that should be raised at this meeting?"

Date of the Next Meeting

Before you close this meeting set the date for the next meeting, unless you have already done this. It's much easier to agree the date of the next meeting while everyone is together. This is also an ideal opportunity for attendees to send their apologies if they know they will be absent.

Exercise: Any Other Business

Now you know when and how to use the 'Any other business' agenda item think about your meetings. How do you currently use 'Any other business'?

Instructions:

Answer the following questions.

1. What do I currently discuss under the 'Any other business' agenda item?

2. Am I currently using 'Any other business' correctly?

3. Do I always accept submissions for 'Any other business'; without checking if the matter is urgent?

4. What am I going to do differently in future?

5. Create an action plan and implement it

For most chairmen/women getting this part of the meeting right is the biggest improvement they make when chairing meetings.

9.3 Closing the Meeting

As the chairperson It's your duty to bring the meeting to a close. Some chairmen/women like to use this as an opportunity for a quick recap. If so:

1. Summarise what has been discussed and agreed

2. Confirm the actions from the meeting

3. Check each action owner understands what is expected of him/her, including the timescale for completing the task

4. Ask each action owner to update the minute taker when their actions are complete

5. If there are any outstanding agenda items check if the proposer wants them to be included for the next meeting. If so, these items should have a priority listing for the next meeting

6. Thank everyone for attending. Always try to end your meetings on a positive note

Note: As this is your meeting you have the power to decide when this meeting closes. It's fine to end a meeting early, but it's bad practice to end a meeting late.

After the meeting has finished you might like to have private word with any latecomers. It's important that attendees realise they must arrive for the start of the meeting. Of course there will be occasions when people are late for reasons beyond their control. Most times it's simply poor time management.

You will know who the habitual latecomers are. Arriving late is very disruptive and needs to be discouraged. If an attendee repeatedly arrives late you may choose to expel them from your meetings. After all they add no value to the meeting if they aren't there.

Exercise: Meeting Review

Do you spend a few minutes reviewing your meetings after the meeting has closed? It's easy to fall into the habit of using the same format, approach and ideas for every meeting.

You may not conduct a self-assessment after every meeting but it's a good exercise to do periodically, at least. Just 5-10 minutes is all that is required for this exercise.

You can do this exercise on your own or with the group.

Instructions:

Consider the following questions.

1. Are your meetings always productive? Do you consistently meet the objectives of your meetings?

2. What can you do to improve the effectiveness of your meetings?

3. Do you consistently have the right people at your meetings?

4. Can your meetings be shortened, or is the right amount of time allocated to them?

5. Do you deal with contentious topics and difficult attendees effectively? Is there anything you can do to improve your assertiveness skills?

6. Is there anything you can do to improve your communication skills?

7. Create an action plan to deal with any possible improvements

Chairing meetings is like any other skill. With practice your skills will get better and better. Accomplished chairmen/women stand out for all the right reasons.

Handy hint: Demonstrating zero tolerance to late arrivals sends out a clear message to everyone. If you don't address the issue of lateness it will become a habit and more people will do it.

10. Communication Skills

Meetings are a common stage where you are on show in front of colleagues, people from other departments and senior personnel. Each one will be judging your ability to communicate effectively. Leaving people with a positive impression could have an influence on your future career prospects.

Effective communication is essential if you want to chair an efficient meeting and appear credible. Careers are often enhanced or blunted in business meetings. Do you perform like someone on the way up, or on the way out?

When listening to what others are saying listen to understand, not to reply. It's important that you understand the different views of the people around the table. This will enable you to resolve differences and build respect and trust.

Always remember to remain impartial and objective. No matter how tempting, don't fall into the trap of asking leading questions or directing discussions towards your preferred outcomes.

If you have nothing to say on a particular agenda item, say nothing. There is nothing to be gained from being a serial over-talker.

When introducing an agenda item provide just enough detail to prompt discussion and questions. Limit your involvement in the discussions. Do not turn into a self-indulgent, pontificating chairperson.

In your role as chairperson you will need a range of communication skills. These include verbal communication, questioning skills, active listening skills, understanding body language and an ability to deal with problem attendees.

10.1 Verbal Communication

Don't be frightened of chairing meetings. Use your voice effectively to sound confident, even if you don't feel it. Keep your voice fairly low; not down in your boots though. If your voice is too high you will sound nervous, which won't inspire confidence.

Pace yourself. Don't talk too fast as others will find it hard to follow what you are saying. Equally don't be too slow as this will make listening to you a painful experience. Just speak at a nice steady, even pace.

When speaking:

1. Keep your tone upbeat

2. Talk to the entire group - move your eyes around the group

3. Use words and phrases that encourage participation. Your role is partially to participate but mostly to facilitate. The hollow sound of silence at meetings is painful for everyone present

10.2 Questioning Skills

After a presentation you may need to ask a few key questions to open up the discussion. Don't use this as an opportunity to get on your soapbox though. Ask real questions. Don't simply ask needless questions for the sake of saying something.

There are six ways for you to ask the group for their views without leading them. These are:

1. Direct a comment or question to one person in the group. If someone has led the discussion or delivered a presentation seek their views first

2. Ask an overhead question. This is when a question it put to the whole group to start the discussion off. This is often used if no-one is leading the discussion for a particular agenda item

3. Ask an overhead question, followed by a directed question. Put a question to the whole group to get everyone thinking. Then follow this up by asking a specific member of the group for his/her views

4. Re-direct a question. If a question is put to you (the chair) and you don't want to or can't answer it, redirect it. Deflect the question back to the rest of the group. Say something like "that's a fair question; what does everyone think about that?"

5. Use a development question to build on the answer from an earlier question. Take someone's comments and move it around the group for other thoughts

6. Ask a rhetorical question. This is a question that doesn't require an answer. It's used to make a point or prompt thinking

Although effective questioning skills are essential they are pointless without answers. Think of yourself as the Jeremy Paxman of the meeting; although a little less aggressive. If a question goes unanswered, ask it again. You may need to rephrase the question as perhaps the group didn't understand it the first time around.

If this doesn't get a response try silence. It's tempting to simply move on with a new question but don't. Generally silence will get someone to speak up. Often the person who finally speaks has a valid point to make. If you hadn't waited patiently you may have missed an important contribution.

10.3 Active Listening Skills

Your role is more about listening than speaking. Some chairmen/women aren't naturally good listeners. If this is your problem, start practicing your listening skills.

Listening is one of the most important skills of a chairperson. How well you listen will have a major impact on your effectiveness as a chairperson. Active listening can be a hard skill to master initially. It's worth the effort as it's a skill that can be used in all areas of your life.

Listening is not the same as hearing. Hearing refers to the sounds that you hear. Listening requires more than that. It requires you to focus on the speaker. It means paying attention, to what is being said and not allowing your mind to wander. It also means noting the choice of words used so you can adapt your words to the speaker's style. Finally, it's about being aware of the non-verbal messages being transmitted.

It takes practice to develop active listening skills. Here are the top 10 tips for demonstrating active listening skills:

1. If possible, face the speaker. Sit up straight and lean slightly forward. Your body language will then suggest that you are listening

2. If you can make eye contact, do so. Don't stare but do try to maintain eye contact long enough to show you are listening

3. Focus on the speaker. Don't allow yourself to be distracted by other people or things going on

4. Either make a comment, nod or even raise your eyebrows to show the speaker you understand what has been said. When chairing meetings you won't always need to prompt further comment as others in the meeting will do this for you

5. Focus on what the speaker is saying. Don't start thinking about what you're going to say next, or looking at the next agenda item. You may need to cut the speaker off. The most effective way to do this is by listening and knowing when to interrupt

6. Stay focused on the discussion. If your mind wanders bring it back to the discussion. After all it's your responsibility to keep the discussions moving forward

7. Try to listen with an open mind. You may not agree with what is being said, but allow everyone to contribute before putting forward your own views

8. Try not to lead the discussions. Your role as chairperson is to remain impartial and objective, no matter how tempting It's to share your views

9. Allow the speaker to make their point before getting defensive. Research shows that, on average, we can hear four times faster than we talk. This means you can process all the information being presented before putting forward your opinion

10. As the chairperson you can ask questions for clarification, or to move the discussion forward. You also need to be able to summarise (link back) what has been said. This is about repeating what has been discussed, but in your own words

10.4 Body Language

Body language or non-verbal communication has a useful part to play in meetings. Never underestimate the power of the nod.

As the chairperson, most people will glance at you when delivering their input. If you want to test this, try the following:

Allow someone to speak and share their views. Wait for them to make eye contact with you and then nod in agreement (as long as you do agree with them). Study the person while he/she is speaking. Notice how many times they look at you for reassurance.

Others in the meeting will probably notice this, and may follow their example. It's a way of acknowledging your role in the meeting. This act also meets a basic human need - that or recognition and reassurance.

This works in the opposite way too. If you nod in disagreement, often the speaker will begin to lose conviction for what they are saying. Therefore, never abuse 'the nod'.

10.5 Dealing With Problem Attendees

Chairing meetings is a good way to test and hone your assertiveness and interpersonal skills. Not every meeting has problem attendees, but It's helpful to know how to handle difficult people.

Most people make an effort to be constructive and effective at meetings. Some, for all sorts of reasons, can be problematic. Here are the primary problem behaviours you may encounter in your meetings. I've also suggested ways to deal with the behaviour.

The Talkative Show-off
This attendee may be genuinely enthusiastic or passionate about the topic. Equally, he/she may just be on a mission to monopolise the discussion. Often this person just wants to demonstrate their knowledge or personal expertise. Unfortunately, you don't have enough meeting time to allow this to continue.

Action
The first step is to take control of the meeting. As soon as the contributor pauses to take breath, pounce. Stem their flow with a positive comment or a word of thanks. Then move the conversation on quickly. Either throw the topic open to the entire group or target a specific person for a comment.

Be prepared for the talkative show-off to strike again. Each time be a little more assertive dealing with him/her until he/she gets the hint.

In extreme cases you may need to have a private word with the offender outside the meeting. Point out that you appreciate their enthusiasm but everyone must be given the opportunity to participate.

The Gusher
This person is also too talkative. Rather than trying to demonstrate their knowledge, this person just wants attention. Often this person wants more than their fair share of time as he/she doesn't like listening.

Action
Meeting time is short and you can't afford to ignore this person. Stem their flow with a positive comment or a word of thanks.

If this doesn't work ask the gusher to summarise his/her point so others can comment. If you don't take control the gusher will hijack your meeting. Others in the group will then switch off; resulting in a less than effective meeting.

The Silent Attendee
The person who sits there and contributes nothing can be just as difficult to deal with. You need to try to understand why. Is this person bored, shy, lacking in self-confidence, inexperienced or has no idea what is being discussed?

Action

It would be easy to simply ignore this person, but this doesn't solve the problem. Often this person has a valuable contribution to make if you can get him/her to speak.

Start by asking direct questions. If he/she is shy this will give them an opportunity to get involved in the discussion without pushing themselves forward.

If this person still resolutely refuses to participate in the meeting speak to him/her after the meeting. If he/she isn't willing to make a contribution in meetings they shouldn't attend future meetings.

This may sound a little harsh, but meetings are expensive. Having non-contributors at meetings is a waste of company time and money.

The Private Meeting

You may find people start their own private discussions in the middle of your meeting. This can be for a variety of reasons, from seeking clarification to plotting. Whatever the reason, this behaviour is an unwelcome distraction.

Action

Don't just ignore the behaviour as it's bound to irritate other attendees. Pause the meeting. This will isolate the chatterers. Often this is all it takes to stop the private meeting.

If the private conversation continues ask if there's a problem, or if something is unclear. Point out the 'only one person talking at a time' rule applies at all times during meetings.

On extremely rare occasions this behaviour will continue. In this case simply ask the offender to leave the meeting. This will stop anyone else behaving in this way.

The Person With a Pet Gripe

This person may have a genuine reason for feeling hard done by, but this is not the place to air it. A meeting is not the place to address grievances as it draws people in who shouldn't be involved. Don't encourage this behaviour.

Action

If the complainer has a genuine gripe, that is relevant to the meeting, can it be resolved with brief discussion? If not, the matter really should be dealt with outside the meeting.

If someone has a genuine and relevant gripe they need to be very clear and specific. The meeting is not a soapbox for complainers.

The Devious or Hidden Agenda Attendee

Occasionally you may be faced with someone who has a hidden agenda. They may use devious behaviour to underplay, disguise or overstate the facts.

Action

It's important for you to learn to read between the lines, or understand the hidden agenda. You can't tackle this effectively until you know what the hidden agenda is.

There are no hard and fast rules for dealing with this situation. Each case needs to be dealt with individually. Ideally you want to stamp this behaviour out quickly. However, sometimes it takes longer-term planning.

I'm Making Excuses

This attendee arrives with excuses for failing to complete his/her actions, print the agenda etc, and not being properly prepared. The most common excuse is lack of time, but some are brazen enough to simply say "I forgot". They make the assumption that you won't pull them up about it.

Action

You can't be seen to allow this to go unchecked as you will appear weak. Remind the attendee, in front of his/her peers, that this is not acceptable. Also point out what your expectations are in future.

Clearly this doesn't solve the problem of the outstanding action(s). Set a new completion date. You could give the task to someone else, but this then lets the attendee off the hook.

The Confrontation Seeker

For whatever reason, you may have someone at your meeting who has a particularly aggressive manner. By adopting a hostile attitude this attendee can disrupt the flow of the meeting. Left unchecked he/she will lower the energy level in the meeting, making it much harder to achieve your objectives.

Action

Remind everyone of the purpose of the meeting and the need to work together to reach agreement. Although this doesn't directly target the perpetrator it does act as a gentle reminder of how to behave appropriately. If the behaviour persists, try to use humour to diffuse the situation.

After the meeting have a private, and less humorous, conversation with the confrontation seeker. It's important that he/she understands that you won't tolerate their behaviour. If the offending behaviour continues you may need to exclude this person from future meetings.

Exercise: Assess Your Communication Skills

If we are completely honest with ourselves, we all like to think we are excellent communicators. In reality, others often don't perceive our communication skills to be as good as we think. The best way to improve any skill is to first identify your strengths and weaknesses.

Don't be overly critical when assessing your skills. Equally, don't bury your head in the sand as this won't fix the problem. As the chairperson you need to have good communication skills in order to facilitate productive meetings.

Read each statement in turn and select the response that most closely relates to you. For example - "I make sure everyone understands what is being discussed in my meetings". Your answer may be 3.

Try not to think about what the right answer is, and just answer truthfully.

1 = Never

2 = Occasionally

3 = Frequently

4 = Always

1. I make sure everyone understands what is being discussed in my meetings

2. I think carefully about what I want to say before I communicate to minimise the chance of misunderstanding

3. I project self-confidence and speak confidently when chairing meetings

4. I listen intently and check I have understood before I reply to other people's comments

5. I make a point of listening even if I find the speaker boring

6. I apply active listening techniques to demonstrate that I'm listening to everything that is being said in my meetings

7. I am constructive when challenging other attendees' views

8. I give everyone a chance to contribute when looking for solutions to problems

9. If I have something to say to someone about their behaviour in a meeting I do this in a one-to-one meeting afterwards

10. I try to exclude personal prejudices when other people are speaking, and ensure everyone feels their contribution was valued

11. I take criticism seriously but not personally

12. I assertively manage those people who try to do all the talking in meetings

13. I understand the dynamics of the personalities involved in my meetings so I can prepare for any difficult behaviour

14. I listen more than I speak in meetings

15. I observe body language of attendees to give me advance warning of problems

16. I know when to be flexible and when to stand my ground

17. I respect other people's opinions even if they differ to mine

Now you have completed this self-assessment add up your score. Your score will be somewhere between 17 and 68. You will find the analysis for your score in the appendices section at the end of the book.

Exercise: Communication Skills Action Plan

Now you've had an opportunity to objectively assess your communication skills you know your strengths and weaknesses. Each of us has communication skills strengths and weaknesses, but knowing them is only half the job. Now create an action plan to address your current weaknesses.

You might also like to identify your strengths and decide how you can use them to mentor other chairmen/women. Mentoring other chairmen/women is a great way to develop your skills and theirs.

Instructions:

Consider the following.

1. What are my strengths as a communicator? Don't be too modest

2. How can I mentor other chairs and share this knowledge with them?

3. What are my communication weaknesses?

4. What am I willing to do to address these?

I recommend you revisit the Assess Your Communication Skills exercise in six months' time and check your scores against today's score. Then revisit your action plan to see if you implemented the changes your planned.

Effective communication is a lifelong skill, and we should be constantly developing and honing our skills.

11. Note Taking and Recording Actions

As the chairperson you may not have time to make your own notes during the meeting. This shouldn't be problematic as long as you give the minute taker the help and support he/she needs during the meeting.

Be aware of how the minute taker is getting on. If your minute taker is struggling with the note taking summarise each discussion for the minutes. Also ensure each action is recorded, has an action owner and a clear timescale for completing the task.

This may slow the meeting down a little initially but it will ensure good quality minutes. Also, you won't have to waste time waiting for the minute taker to catch up.

Never try to take on the role of chairperson and minute taker. This will slow the meeting down unnecessarily. Furthermore, you will probably not perform successfully in either role.

Don't be tempted to give yourself all the actions. Some chairmen/women do fall into this trap. If you overload yourself with actions and then fail to complete them all you will harm your personal credibility.

It's far more efficient to share the actions amongst all the attendees. This ensures that no-one ends up with an unduly heavy workload as a result of the meeting.

Actions can only be allocated to people present at the meeting. The action owner may choose to delegate the task to someone outside the meeting, which is fine. As far as the minutes are concerned the action remains the responsibility of the action owner identified in the meeting. The ownership can't be delegated.

12. Approving and Issuing the Minutes

A perk of being the chairperson is you don't have a huge amount of work to do following the meeting. The minute taker is the person with the biggest workload.

You are expected to provide any help and support the minute taker needs to compile clear, concise and accurate minutes. Your role is also checking and verifying the minutes once they have been drafted.

As the chairperson, you are also expected to provide help and support to any attendee needing assistance to complete their actions.

12.1 Styles of Minutes

If your organisation doesn't have a policy on the preferred style of minutes you can select the style you prefer. Note: summary minutes are suitable for most business meetings.

To help you choose the style of minutes for your meeting I've included a précis of each style.

Summary Minutes
These are the most commonly used style of minutes. They provide more information than action point minutes, but less than verbatim minutes.

Summary minutes include a short description (summary) of the discussion that took place. This is generally no more than five sentences. They also contain details of all actions, action owners and the completion date.

This style of minutes provides all the essential information without being overly long.

Verbatim Minutes
Verbatim minutes are generally created when a very detailed and accurate record of a meeting is required. You will need to include minutes for each sub-heading as well as the main headings.

As you would expect, these minutes are lengthy. In this case verbatim doesn't always means 'word-for-word'. However it does mean everything that was discussed during the meeting. Unfortunately, this is unavoidable.

Any part of the discussion that is particularly important, controversial or sensitive may be captured word-for-word. Advise the minute taker if you wish any of the discussion to be captured word-for-word.

Verbatim minutes are most commonly created for formal meetings. They are also used for disciplinary hearings or meetings following a health and safety incident. If you want verbatim minutes, make this clear to the minute taker before the meeting starts. It will be impossible to do this this afterwards.

Action Point Minutes

These are hardly minutes at all as they don't contain any information about the discussion that took place. Anyone reading these minutes will have no idea of the discussion that took place. As the name suggests, the only information captured relates to the actions. Record details of the action, action owner and completion date.

This style of minutes is commonly used for project planning meetings and informal meetings. If you only need to record the actions, this style of minutes is ideal.

12.2 Approving the Minutes

The minute taker will create a draft set of minutes for you to review and approve. This should be done within two working days of the meeting. Even though the minute taker creates the minutes you are the owner of this document. You are responsible for the accuracy of the minutes.

When reviewing the minutes you are checking them for accuracy. This is not an opportunity for you to alter the minutes because you don't like the writing style or content. Although minutes are generally boring, they are meant to be an accurate and factual record of the meeting.

Do not add anything to the minutes that wasn't discussed at the meeting. If something was discussed but has been missed out of the minutes then this should be included. Reviewing the minutes should never be viewed as carte blanche to change the content.

It's good practice to approve the minutes within four working days of the meeting. The minutes' should then be issued straightaway (certainly no later than five working days after the meeting). You don't need to issue the minutes as this is the minute taker's responsibility. However, you should approve the minutes before they are issued.

Note: If you don't authorise issuing the minutes in a timely manner most people won't bother reading them. After five working days most people have put the meeting to the back of their mind.

It's common for attendees to wait for the minutes before completing their actions from the meeting. If the minutes are issued late the actions may not be completed by the next meeting. In some cases the actions won't be completed at all.

12.3 Who Should Have a Copy of the Minutes?

As this was your meeting you are the owner of the minutes. This means you have discretion over who can and can't have a copy of the minutes. Of course there are some rules regarding who is entitled to a copy of the minutes.

Anyone who was invited to the meeting is entitled to a copy of the minutes. This includes those people who sent apologies or failed to attend. If the minutes contain sensitive or confidential information you may choose to only issue them to regular attendees. Ask the minute taker to include a note about the confidential nature in the covering email.

People who weren't invited to the meeting are not automatically entitled to a copy of the minutes. This is regardless of their seniority in the organisation. Anyone wanting a copy of the minutes should seek your permission, not simply ask the minute taker for a copy.

Exercise: Review of the Meeting and Post-meeting Stage

You have now worked through running the meeting and approving and issuing the minutes. Now is a good time to review how you got on.

Instructions:

1. Review you answers from the 'Your Strengths and Weaknesses as a Chairperson' exercise in chapter 4. Has your opinion changed regarding your strengths and weaknesses as a chairperson?

2. If yes, what has changed?

3. Do you generally alter the draft minutes? If so, why do you alter them?

4. Do you give priority to reviewing and approving the minutes? If not, do you now recognise the importance of this task?

5. Are you clear in your instructions to the minute taker about who can and can't have a copy of the minutes?

6. Can you identify any ways to improve the process of approving and issuing the minutes? If so, what are you going to do differently in future?

This exercise is an opportunity for you to reflect on what you currently do, and find ways to make you even more efficient.

13. Freedom of Information Act

The Freedom of Information Act 2000 gives UK citizens the right to ask any public body for all the information they have on any subject they choose. The Freedom of Information (Scotland) Act 2002 covers the public bodies that the Holyrood parliament has jurisdiction over.

The Freedom of Information and Privacy Act is the United States equivalent. For other countries type https://en.wikipedia.org/wiki/Freedom_of_information_laws_by_country. Select the country from the list available.

The media frequently uses this right to obtain information that forms the basis of news stories. Unless there is a good reason not to, the organisation must provide the information within 20 working days.

Anyone can make a request for information, and you can ask for any information you like. There are no restrictions on age, nationality or where you live. Some information may be withheld to protect various interests that are allowed by the Act. If information is withheld the public authority must tell you why they have not shared this information.

You can also ask for any personal information the organisation holds about you. If you ask for information about yourself, then your request will be dealt with under the Data Protection Act 1998.

From a minute taker's point of view the Freedom of Information Act and the Data Protection Act can present a major challenge. When creating minutes carefully consider how much information should be recorded (particularly if you work in the public sector).

13.1 The Public Sector

If you work in the public sector be aware of the impact the Freedom of Information Act may have on your role. We are only dealing with the Act in respect of meetings and minute taking. You will need to do your own research to find out how the Act impacts your role more broadly.

The Freedom of Information Act applies to all public bodies. These include:

1. Government departments. The list is extensive. Type 'How to make a freedom of information request' into your search engine for details of the departments

2. Local authorities and councils

74

3. Schools colleges and universities

4. Health trusts, hospitals and doctors' surgeries

5. Publicly owned companies

6. Publicly funded museums

7. The police

13.2 What is Covered by the Freedom of Information Act?

The Freedom of Information Act requires every public authority to have a 'publication scheme'. This has to be approved by the Information Commissioner's Officer (ICO), and has to include the information covered by the scheme.

In short, this scheme means that certain classes of information must be routinely available to the public. This includes policies and procedures, minutes of meetings, annual reports and financial information.

If you would like to know more about what is covered by the Freedom of Information Act, please refer to the Information Commissioner's website (http://ico.org.uk).

13.3 Exempt Information

As I've already stated anyone can request information held by a public authority. This doesn't mean you will always receive all the information you ask for though. If there is a good reason to refuse the request, some information can be withheld.

There are three reasons why public authorities may refuse an entire request. These reasons are:

1. It would cost too much or take too many staff to deal with the request

2. The request is deemed to be vexatious

3. The request repeats a previous request from the same person

There are also various reasons for a public authority only providing limited information. If you would like to know more please refer to the Information Commissioner's website (http://ico.org.uk).

Even though you may not have to disclose a full copy of your minutes do take care when minuting discussions.

13.4 Useful Websites

If you work in a role where your meetings and minutes may be subject to the Freedom of Information Act you may find the following websites helpful.

The Freedom of Information Act:

United Kingdom - http://www.gov.uk

Scotland - http://www.scotland.gov.uk

United States - http://www.foia.gov/

The Information Commission:

United Kingdom - http://www.ico.gov.uk/

Scotland - http://www.itspublicknowledge.info

United States Information Agency - http://www.dosfan.lib.uic.edu/usia/

Handy hint: If your minutes contain confidential information make a reference indicating where this can be found. If you receive a freedom of information request you will be able to identify and remove the confidential information easily.

14. Conclusion

There is more to being a good chairperson than just turning up and running the meeting. As a chairperson, your role starts as soon as you make the decision to have a meeting. In varying degrees you have a role to play at every stage of the meeting. You are the owner of this meeting, from identifying the need for a meeting until the next meeting.

Effective and efficient meetings can be summarised by the five P's. These are - preparation, purpose, process, performance and pay-off. Treat this as your chairperson's checklist.

1. Preparation

This involves first deciding that a meeting is the best option. Never decide to have a meeting just because it seems like a good idea.

Next think about who should attend, why, when, where and what. When and where is not only the meeting date and venue. When also includes issuing the agenda and other documents well in advance of the meeting date. It also includes when the minutes should be issued.

Finally, think about what information you need to give attendees to enable them to prepare for the meeting. If people don't know what is expected of them they can't prepare properly. Poor preparation leads to poor meetings.

2. Purpose

As you have decided that a meeting is either necessary or the best option, think purpose. If you can't easily define the purpose of your meeting you don't need one.

Obviously you need to know the purpose of the meeting but so does everyone else who is being invited. As the chairperson it's your responsibility to ensure everyone is properly briefed.

3. Process

Think about how the meeting should be conducted. A meeting doesn't have to be a series of discussions to address the agenda items. Meetings can include presentations or skills building.

Skills building can also be team building exercises that pull the group together. Skills building can involve giving other people the opportunity to chair the meeting or be the minute taker. Alternatively, you could delegate the responsibility for time-keeping.

If you're planning to give someone a role at your meeting tell them in advance. Never spring skills building opportunities on people at the start of the meeting. This is a recipe for failure.

4. Performance
No one likes criticism, but constructive feedback can be useful. Well delivered feedback can help you to enhance your personal skillset and effectiveness.

Periodically consider asking someone to appraise your performance. Obviously this needs to be someone whose opinion you value, and someone who is prepared to be honest.

After meetings spend a couple of minutes reflecting on what went well and what could be improved.

5. Pay-off
Finally, there needs to be a pay-off. Otherwise meetings become an expensive waste of time. Ask yourself the following three quick questions:

1. What is the pay-off for the attendees?

2. What is the pay-off for the organisation?

3. What is the pay-off for me personally?

How often have you heard the expression "a meeting is an event where minutes are kept and hours are lost?" Unfortunately, this comment is usually attributed to the ineffective skills of the person chairing the meeting.

By now you probably feel you know all about chairing meetings. Why not test your knowledge with this quick quiz?

Exercise: Chairing Meetings Quiz

1. Who can decide whether someone should attend the meeting or not?

2. Does everyone need to attend the entire meeting?

3. Should you delay the start of a meeting until everyone has arrived?

4. Is it better to finish the agenda or finish the meeting on time?

5. Should the chairperson take sides in meetings?

6. What should you do if you have strong feelings about one of the agenda items, and want to actively participate in the discussion?

7. Is everyone at the meeting expected to contribute to the discussions?

8. Why is the 'Welcome and Introductions' part of the meeting so important?

9. Should you accept every agenda item request? If not, how do you decide what to accept and what to reject?

10. What should appear on the chairperson's agenda that doesn't appear on the attendees' copy of the agenda?

You will find the answers to these questions in the Appendices section at the end of the book.

As I've said previously, every meeting needs a chairperson, or someone to take charge of the meeting. Without someone to carefully guide and direct the meeting it's likely to be a free-for-all.

The benefits of a well-directed meeting include:

1. Better focus on the objectives of the meeting

2. Constructive discussion that is relevant to the agenda items

3. Valid discussion prior to making any decisions

4. All sides of an argument can be aired in a measured way

5. Matters can be discussed in a business-like way, which is generally a less argumentative approach

6. All actions are recorded, along with the action owner and a completion date

If you get the meeting off to a good start you have a much better chance of the meeting going well. If you get off to a poor start you're unlikely to turn things around. As with everything, first impressions count.

Although few chairmen/women do it, we should conduct a personal review after every meeting. This is the best way to ensure that future meetings can be improved. There's no need to involve other people in the evaluation, but consider the following points:

1. Were the objectives of the meeting clear and measurable?

2. Were these valid reasons to meet?

3. Did we meet the objectives?

4. Was the agenda clear and relevant?

5. Were the agenda and any supporting documents issued at least five working days before the meeting? The timescale will be shorter for weekly meetings

6. Was the meeting room suitable for the meeting (think room size, location, accessibility, noise etc)?

7. Were the right people invited to the meeting?

8. Did everyone make a valid contribution?

9. Were all discussions constructive and relevant to the agenda items?

10. Were all the actions from the previous meeting completed?

11. Was the timing well managed?

12. Did the meeting start and finish on time?

13. Did I remain impartial throughout the meeting?

14. What could I do better at future meetings?

If you have identified areas for improvement create an action plan.

Everyone recognises and admires the skills of a competent chairperson. Aim to be the best chairperson you can be. This is a very useful skill, particularly if you have career aspirations.

You have now worked your way through the entire meeting cycle. You may like to do the case study exercise below. The case study is written from an observers prospective. It covers some very common issues that you may recognise from meetings you attend as a chairperson or attendee.

Exercise: Chairing Meetings Case Study

Overview:
You have recently started working at 'The Only Way Is Up Ltd'; a business consultancy that employs 40 staff. You are employed as the PA to the Chief Executive. He formed the company five years ago.

The Chief Executive confirmed that he's an experienced meetings chairman and attendee. He recognises that good practice protocols exist but accepts that he doesn't always implement them. Some of his team don't know that protocol exists for meetings and minute taking.

Each month the Chief Executive has a meeting with his two fellow Directors, the Sales and Marketing Manager and 10 Sales and Marketing

Consultants. The Chief Executive is always the chairman of this meeting. The aim of this meeting is to review how the business is getting on. The objectives for each meeting are:

1. Focus on existing customers (identify if we've lost any customers since the last meeting)

2. Is there anything we could have done to keep them?

3. Discuss new customers gained since the last meeting

4. Identify potential new customers and how we might secure their business

5. Consider ways to raise our profile and market ourselves better

As part of the meeting the group discusses customer queries, sales techniques that are or aren't working, and any areas of weakness in terms of performance. This is used to move the business forward.

This is your first meeting. You're an observer at this meeting so you can see how they operate. The Chief Executive has asked for your feedback at the end of the meeting. As a fresh pair of eyes, he thinks you may be able to see things they don't see.

The departing PA is the minute taker for this meeting. She is an excellent shorthand secretary and prides herself on her ability to capture everything that is said.

Attendees:
Chief Executive - Dennis Jackson (DJ)
Outgoing PA - Pamela Partridge (PP)
Director - Sara Higgins (SH)
Finance Director - Freddie Fiscal (FF)
Sales and Marketing Manager - Alexandros Stavros (AS)
Sales and Marketing Consultant - Rajesh Kumani (RK)
Sales and Marketing Consultant - Poppy Frankenstone (PF)
Sales and Marketing Consultant - Betty-Jean McBricker (BJM)
Sales and Marketing Consultant - Melville Muchrocks (MM)
Sales and Marketing Consultant - Lan Patel (LP)
Sales and Marketing Consultant - Hazel Sheppard (HS)
Sales and Marketing Consultant - Hugo Williams (HW)
Sales and Marketing Consultant - Sachiko Jaggers (SJ)
Sales and Marketing Consultant - Ricky Cobblehoff (RC)
Sales and Marketing Consultant - Lucy Chan (LC)

Actions:
The actions agreed during this meeting were:

1. We've lost one of our oldest clients in the last month. They said they could no longer afford our services. AS has an action to speak to the customer and see if we can get them back again

2. Everyone is to bring last month's and this month's sales reports to the next meeting

3. Each of the Sales Consultants has been asked to come up with a plan for getting three new clients before the end of the year. Alexandros Stavros is to work with the team and create an action plan for discussion at the next meeting

Your Observations:
Your observations from the meeting are:

1. The chairman arrived 10 minutes late. No-one commented or seemed to mind

2. As the chairman was late he skipped the 'Welcome and administration' agenda item. He was keen to make up some of the lost time

3. The agenda was handed out at the start of the meeting

4. Melville Muchrocks and Lan Patel didn't turn up, but didn't send their apologies either. No one knew why they were absent. Everyone else was present

5. Two errors were found in last month's minutes. The minute taker made a hand-written note on her copy of the previous minutes. She didn't record this in the minutes for today's meeting

6. The chairman signed the copy with the hand-written amendments

7. Various conversations were going on during the meeting. The chairman ignored this. The attendees talking amongst themselves made the task of minute taking hard work

8. Most of the attendees had forgotten to bring copies of last month's sales reports. The chairman decided to adjourn this item until the next meeting

9. Part way through the meeting Pamela, the outgoing PA, was asked to serve coffee. No-one took any notes while this was happening so there was a gap in the notes for the minutes

10. One of Ricky Cobblehoff's actions from last month's meeting hasn't been completed. There was no satisfactory explanation for this. This wasn't addressed

11. You notice that the first action doesn't have a completion date

12. The minute taker has captured everything that was said during the meeting

Post-meeting:
After the meeting the chairman asked you what you thought of your first meeting with 'The Only Way Is Up Ltd'. He recognises that the company's meetings are sometimes chaotic. He said this was as a result of the company growing faster than expected.

They didn't have the funds to provide formal meetings and minute taking training for staff when the company started. Now we're too busy to send staff on a formal training course as everyone is needed to cope with the workload.

The Chief Executive thinks it's time for the company to become more professional in the way it handles meetings. He recognises that the company if probably wasting time and money in some instances. He wants to start with this meeting and then roll out new working practices for all company meetings.

Your Task:
The Chief Executive knows you are an experienced meeting secretary and minute taker. He would value your feedback on the following. The Chief Executive would like you to present your findings in a short report. How you choose to present your report is up to you.

1. Explain what was wrong with the meeting you attended

2. Explain what the chairman could do to be more effective in his role

3. Confirm what the chairperson is responsible for when planning the meeting

4. Confirm what support the chairperson should be giving the meeting secretary and the minute taker

4. All the company's meetings are monthly. Confirm the timescale for issuing the agenda and minutes

5. Confirm whether the chairman needs to approve the agenda and minutes before they are issued

6. Suggest the best style of agenda for future company meetings, and explain why you have chosen this one

7. Suggest the best style of minutes for future meetings, and explain why you have chosen this one

8. To test your knowledge and expertise, the chief executive would like you to create a separate document with the actions from this meeting

9. Create an action plan for implementing these changes. When doing this, think about the best way to get everyone to engage with the process of change

This case study is an opportunity to reflect on what you already knew and to confirm what you've learnt from this book.

I hope this book has provided you with some little nuggets of information that will help you hone your 'chairing skills'. If you have any comments, observations or questions about chairing meetings I would be delighted to hear from you.

Shepherd Creative Learning welcomes feedback, postive or negative. If you would like to get in touch with us our email address is shepherdcreativelearning@gmail.com.

The final word goes to Eli Broad (a renowned business leader who built two Fortune 500 companies). "I don't like to spend time in endless meetings talking about stuff that isn't going to get anything done. I have meetings, but they're short, prompt and to the point." This is good advice for anyone who chairs meetings.

15. Terms

The terms in this chapter can relate to formal, business and informal meetings.

Absent - These are the people who were expected to attend the meeting. They didn't turn up or send their apologies

Any other business - This is an agenda item for emergency use only. This is an opportunity to discuss urgent matters that came to light after the agenda was issued

Attendees - This can be anyone attending the meeting. This includes the chairperson, minute taker, attendees, visitors or observers

Chairperson - The person running the meeting. This is not necessarily the most senior person in the room

Chairperson's brief - This is also known as the chairperson's agenda. It's simply a more detailed agenda than the version issued to the other attendees

Contributors - These are also referred to as attendees. These can be people who attended all or part of the meeting. As the name suggests they are expected to contribute to the meeting in some way. Anyone who doesn't contribute and isn't there as an observer should leave/not attend in future

Declarations of interest - These are a potential conflict of interest relating to one (or more) of the agenda items. Declarations of interest should be declared at the start of the meeting

In attendance - This term is used for formal meetings only. The term refers to people present, who aren't board members

Matters arising - These are the actions from the previous meeting. Ideally each action should be closed at the current meeting, not carried forward to future meetings

Meeting secretary - The person creating and issuing the agenda and other documents for discussion at the meeting. Note: often the meeting secretary and minute taker are the same person

Minutes of the previous meeting - These are the minutes from the previous meeting. At the current meeting, these minutes will be adopted or amended

Minute taker - The person responsible for taking notes in the meeting and creating and issuing the minutes

Observers - People who have been invited to observe the meeting. Only the chairperson should invite observers. Observers are not permitted to participate in the meeting, but they should be there for a specific reason e.g. future minute taker

Substitutes - These are people who are deputising for a regular member of the group, who is unable to attend. Substitutes are expected to participate in the discussions are far as possible. Otherwise there is no point in them attending the meeting

Visitors - These are people who don't normally attend the meeting. They have usually been invited to deliver a presentation, lead a discussion or contribute to a specific agenda item. Visitors aren't normally expected to stay for the entire meeting

16. Appendices

In this chapter you will find the answers to the exercises earlier in the book.

16.1 Exercise: The 7 Key Skills of a Good Chairperson - Answers

Here are the answers to The 7 Key Skills of a Good Chairperson in chapter 1.

1. Good time management skills

2. An excellent communicator

3. Assertiveness skills

4. Ability to ensure decisions are made during the meeting

5. Accurately record actions

6. Flexible approach

7. Impartial

16.2 Exercise: Evaluate Your Skills as a Chairperson - Answers

So how did your fare? Here are the answers to the Evaluate Your Skills as a Chairperson exercise in chapter 4.

Now you have your score from this exercise, read the analysis below. This evaluation is not intended as a stick to beat you with. Only by understanding your weaknesses can you tackle them. Use this information in the spirit it's intended:

Score 12-24:
Clearly there is some work to do if you want to become an effective chairperson. Perhaps you are new to the role or have never received any formal training. Hopefully the information contained in this book will help improve your chairing skills.

Do the follow-on exercise and identify your strengths and weaknesses as a chairperson. Identify the bad habits you are currently adopting or things you can do to improve your chairing skills. Create and implement an action plan. I recommend you do this exercise again in three months' time to see how your skills have improved. You may find it helpful to find a mentor.

It's important to recognise what you do well, not simply identify your failings. This will help to keep you motivated to improve your chairing skills.

Score 25-36:
You have some strengths and some weaknesses as a chairperson. Do the follow-on exercise and identify what your strengths and weaknesses are.

It's important to recognise what you do well, not simply identify your failings. Pat yourself on the back for the good practices you've adopted. You may like to share this knowledge with other chairmen/women to help them improve their skills.

Identify your weak points and then create and implement an action plan. Repeat this exercise in three months' time to see how your skills have improved.

Score: 37-48:
You should feel proud of your skills as a chairperson. You may like to mentor other less experienced or less capable chairmen/women to help them improve.

Also take the opportunity to see what more you can do to further improve your chairing skills. You may feel you have nothing to learn from reading this book now, but hopefully you will find some little nuggets to further enhance your skills.

16.3 Exercise: My Self Confidence - Analysis

Here is the analysis from the My Self Confidence exercise in chapter 9.

Mostly yes:
You may or may not be confident but you are good at giving the impression of confidence. This is a valuable management skill, not just for meetings.

Look at the questions where your response was no or sometimes. What can you do to change these responses to yes?

Mostly no:
You appear to lack confidence, which won't inspire confidence from the people attending the meetings.

If attendees don't have confidence in your ability as a chairperson they will probably be more difficult or challenging during the meeting. It would be in your own interests to:

1. Attend an assertiveness or confidence building course

2. Find someone to mentor you

3. Start working on each question where you answered no

You've probably heard the expression 'fake it until it becomes a reality'. This is one example where that rule applies. If you keep telling yourself you are a confident and effective chairperson it will become a reality eventually.

Mostly sometimes:
You clearly have the skills and confidence, but probably need to keep reminding yourself. Your approach to chairing meetings is probably inconsistent currently. This is doing nothing to promote your personal brand as an effective chairperson.

Look at the questions where your response was 'sometimes'. What can you do to change these responses to yes?

Depending upon how frequently your chair meetings I recommend you revisit this exercise in three or six months' time.

16.4 Exercise: Assess Your Communication Skills - Answers

Here are the answers to the Evaluate Your Skills as a Chairperson exercise in chapter 10.

Now you have your score from this exercise, read the analysis below. This evaluation is not intended as a stick to beat you with. Only by understanding your weaknesses can you tackle them. Use this information in the spirit it's intended:

Score 17 – 33:
You are not communicating effectively in your meetings. Listen to feedback, practice your observation skills and try to learn from your mistakes. You may like to find a mentor to help you develop some good chairing skills

Score 34 – 50:

Your communication skills are patchy – sometimes good and sometimes poor. Identify your weaknesses and work on these. This will improve your overall performance as a chairperson

Score 51 – 68:
You communicate very well but remember that you can never communicate too much. Further develop your communication skills by inviting feedback from the people who attend your meetings. As you're an accomplished chairperson you might like to consider mentoring those who need to improve their chairing skills

16.5 Exercise: Chairing Meetings Quiz - Answers

Here are the answers to the Chairing Meetings Quiz in chapter 14.

1. Only the chairperson has the right to approve the list of attendees for the meeting. Others can request attendance at the meeting, but the decision is at your discretion

2. Answer - No. There is no benefit asking people to attend the entire meeting if they have nothing to contribute. It's common for visitors to just attend for a specific agenda items. Regular attendees normally stay for the whole meeting, even though they may not participate in every discussion

3. Always start your meetings on time, even if some of the attendees are missing. If you wait the message this sends is 'late arrivals are more important than those who arrived on time'. Don't recap for latecomers

4. Always finish the meeting on time. Remember, everyone will have other meetings or tasks planned. Agenda items not completed today should be given priority at the next meeting

5. Answer - No. As the chairperson you should remain neutral during the discussions. As chairperson, you do have the casting vote if it becomes necessary. You should cast your vote after everyone else so you can't be accused of trying to influence the outcome

6. If you have strong feelings about one of the agenda items, and want to actively participate in the discussion ask someone else to act as chairperson for the relevant agenda item. This will allow you to participate as an attendee, rather than the chairperson

7. Answer - Yes. The only people who aren't permitted to contribute are observers. Everyone else should make a contribution or leave

8. The 'Welcome and Introductions' part of the meeting is important because it sets the scene for the meeting. It's an opportunity for you to state the aim and objectives of the meeting and assert yourself as chair. Attendees will use this time to decide whether the meeting is worth their time. Even in meetings, first impressions count

9. You don't have to include every agenda item just because you've been asked to do so. Each item must be relevant to the rest of the agenda and the majority of the attendees. If not, suggest it should be discussed outside the meeting. Do tell people if you decide not to include their agenda item though

10. The chairperson's agenda is more detailed than the version issued to everyone else. It may include timings and notes about expected outcomes. It could include and any other information that will help you when discussing the agenda item

My final word on meetings ... "no grand idea was ever born in a conference, but a lot of foolish ideas have died there" - Anonymous.

Thank you for choosing to read my book.

Printed in Great Britain
by Amazon